ALSO BY JONATHAN SCHELL

The Village of Ben Suc (1967)
The Military Half (1968)
The Time of Illusion (1976)
The Fate of the Earth (1982)
The Abolition (1984)

History in
Sherman Park

HISTORY IN SHERMAN PARK

*An American Family and
the Reagan-Mondale Election*

Jonathan Schell

ALFRED A. KNOPF   NEW YORK

1 9 8 7

THIS IS A BORZOI BOOK
PUBLISHED BY ALFRED A. KNOPF, INC.

The contents of this book originally appeared in *The New Yorker*.

Library of Congress Cataloging-in-Publication Data
Schell, Jonathan, [date]   History in Sherman Park.

1. Presidents—United States—Election—1984—Public opinion. 2. United States—Politics and government—1981– Public opinion. 3. Public opinion—Wisconsin—Milwaukee. 5. Sherman Park (Milwaukee, Wis.)—Politics and government—Public opinion. 6. Milwaukee (Wis.)—Politics and government—Public opinion.
I. Title.
E879.S34   1987   324.973'0927   87-45239
ISBN 0-394-56300-X

Manufactured in the United States of America
FIRST EDITION

For Wally, with love

Acknowledgments

I would like to thank the Public Agenda Foundation for its generous assistance in helping me find my way to the Gapolinsky family. I owe special thanks to John Doble, Vice-President of the Foundation, for indispensable advice and for companionship in travels around the country.

History in Sherman Park

ONE EVENING IN early September of 1984, I pulled up in front of the home of Gina and William Gapolinsky, in the Milwaukee neighborhood known as Sherman Park. (I have changed their names, the names of some others, and certain details in this book to protect their privacy.) I was there to talk with them about the Presidential election, which had got its start on Labor Day. In every election season, the candidates, the candidates' supporters, the reporters, the commentators, and others in and around the campaigns pour forth their messages—speeches, political advertisements, press conferences, leaks, articles, editorials—hoping to cast light (or to obfuscate), to clarify (or to muddle), to inform, to argue, to persuade, to charm, to dazzle: to win. I wanted to go to some particular place in America where this bombardment was arriving—where some individual voters were making up their minds whom to vote for as they went about the business of their lives. And, having put myself there, I wanted to look back at the campaigns and their interpreters —and to reflect on what was going on. I knew that on the basis of my talks with these people I could not make political generalizations of the kind that political polls allow, but I wanted to find out things that a poll could not reveal. Instead of finding out a little about a lot of votes, I wanted to find out everything I could about a handful of votes. After all, I thought, it was here—in the minds of individual voters —that an election, in the last analysis, took place. As in every campaign, the full range of issues handled by government was being presented for judgment and decision; among innumerable other issues were whether we would go to war or remain at peace, raise taxes or lower them, protect the natural environment or despoil it, expand individual liberties or shrink them, undermine foreign governments or leave them alone, regulate industry or unleash it, increase aid to the poor and disadvantaged or cut it back. And, because the election was taking place in the nuclear age, also at issue was the question of how the species could best assure its survival, and even whether it could survive at all; so the continuation of human life, too, was—fantastically—at issue in the election. In other political systems, those issues are handed over to the few for decision, or to just one person —to a revolutionary council, to a politburo, to a president-for-life, to a sovereign, to a king—but under our system it is the citizens who decide. Citizens, it is true, have much on their minds besides politics, and may take little or no interest in an election or in the issues raised in it (in 1984, as it turned out, nearly 47 percent of the voting-age population did not bother to vote); or they may be swayed or pressured to vote one way or another by powerful forces in the society; or they may be offered such restricted choices in the first place that their true will never has a chance to be expressed. Yet the fact remains that, however the decision whom to vote for is arrived at, it is the people in the voting booths who decide which person takes office. At the very least, if the powerful forces wish to have their way they are forced to exert their influence through the minds of the citizens, and if the citizens, for whatever reason, rebel, their will prevails. So if in going to Sherman Park to talk with Gina and Bill Gapolinsky I was in one sense seeking out people at the bottom of the political hierarchy—people far from the centers of influence and power, on the receiving end of the government's decisions—I was in another sense seeking out the people who, under our system, are at the very pinnacle of power. It was not the President, or the senators, or the representatives who would decide, ultimately, whether taxes would be raised or lowered, whether the poor would be helped or abandoned, whether the world would end or go on; it was Gina and Bill. Whatever their level of interest, or concern, or information, their decisions were the ones that stuck. They were the American sovereign. They were the American king.

In the campaign so far, the polls declared, President Reagan had established a wide lead. At the Republican National Convention, in late August, he had framed the election as a choice between not merely two programs for governing America but two general moods, or temperamental inclinations—"optimism" on the Republican side and "pessimism" on the Democratic side. The Democrats, he said upon arriving in Dallas, offered the country "defeatism, decline, dependency, doom, and despair." Their very fear of these ills beginning with the letter "d," he seemed to be saying, would bring the ills on. The Democrats, he said in his acceptance speech, were pessimists who undermined "the confidence and optimism about the future that has made us unique in the world." They preached that "decline was inevitable," Representative Jack Kemp said at the Convention, because there were forces "beyond our control," and that "America had reached its limits." It was anything but surprising, then, Senator Paul Laxalt said, that under President Carter the nation had been "humbled at home, humiliated abroad." And the Soviet leaders, for their part, United Nations Ambassador Jeane Kirkpatrick said, had "moved with boldness and skill to exploit their new advantages." But then, the preamble to the Republican platform said, there had begun a "new dawn of the American spirit." Under Ronald Reagan, in just "four short years" (Laxalt), America had become well. The economy roared ahead, the Russians fell back, and America, "respected" once again, was restored to its role as "a model for other nations" (Kemp).

In the weeks following the Convention, the Reagan campaign ran a richly atmospheric series of television advertisements that were much admired by people in the business and whose chief aim seemed to be to create a climate of national well-being and happiness—even of euphoria—and to link this with the Reagan Administration. One ad that was widely commented upon announced, in a soothing deep male voice, "It's morning again in America," and consisted almost entirely of pleasing scenes of American life offered in succession—a tugboat moving up a river at dawn, a beautiful young couple getting married, and more. Reagan also made a series of campaign appearances carefully designed to lend themselves to the brief, impressionistic coverage characteristic of television. In one of these, the President attended a birthday party for the celebrated and loved country-and-Western star Roy Acuff at the Grand Ole Opry, in Nashville, Tennessee, and, against the backdrop of a gigantic American flag, helped Acuff cut a giant birthday cake.

Against this skillful, unified presentation of a happy, confident, optimistic country being led by a strong leader, the Democratic candidate, former Vice-President Walter Mondale, sought to pit a series of quite detailed criticisms of specific policies of the Reagan Administration. He often pointed out that Reagan had failed to conclude any agreements with the Soviet Union on the control of nuclear arms and that during his Presidency the federal budget deficit had risen from $74 billion to $185 billion. He accused the Administration of neglecting the environment, of trying to reverse progress in the field of civil-rights law and legislation, of condoning human-rights abuses by right-wing regimes abroad. In a controversial recommendation at the Democratic National Convention, in mid-July, he also proposed that taxes be raised to cut the budget deficit. So far, however, he had not pulled these criticisms together into any overall theme, much less created an infectious mood of the kind that had been created by the Reagan campaign. At the Convention, he advocated a "new realism" for the Democratic Party, but the idea did not catch on and was soon forgotten. He tried on occasion to boil down his list of criticisms into something more readily appealing, but managed only to produce a shorter list: "a safer America," "fairness," and "a more competitive America." In early September, he suggested to a reporter that the central message of his campaign was going to be "what kind of people we are"— whether idealistic or selfish, compassionate or cruel—but no concerted or coordinated effort was made to give that idea prominence.

If Reagan seemed to slight policy in favor of mood, Mondale at times seemed to get lost in the details of policy. Mondale's early campaign appearances were marked by mistakes. His first official day of campaigning, on Labor Day, became a cross-country demonstration of error and mishap. In the morning, in New York, he showed up for the Labor Day parade before the parade had attracted many spectators, and so was forced to march along sparsely lined streets in front of the television cameras; at midday, he flew to Merrill, Wisconsin, where his audience was rained on before he spoke; and in the evening he arrived so late for a rally at Long Beach, California, that the event could not be covered in the evening news. The manner and method of the two campaigns soon became as much of an issue in the election as any of the supposedly substantial issues mentioned in the candidates' speeches. President Reagan's campaign was praised for its businesslike efficiency and its public-relations creativity and skill but faulted for its lack of concentration on issues, while Mondale's campaign was praised for its concentration on issues but faulted for its inefficiency and its ineptness. In press commentary, it became something of a cliché to say that many people who agreed with Mondale on most of the issues were going to vote for Reagan anyway. Commentators had remarked that Reagan seemed to be shielded by a coat of political Teflon that mysteriously protected him from having to pay any political price with the public for errors of his Administration. Now it was beginning to look as if the Teflon protected him from rival candidates as well. A destructive synergism seemed to be at work in the Mondale campaign. The Republicans had portrayed him as the candidate of "decline"; now the point seemed to be illustrated daily by the waning popularity of his candidacy. And while Mondale, seen as both the apostle and the exemplar of defeat, sank in his vortex of failure Reagan seemed to ascend on the spiral of success.

THE GAPOLINSKYS' HOUSE occupied a small lot on a tree-lined street on the north side of Milwaukee. It had two stories—the first of brick, the second of aluminum siding, which overhung the brick by a few inches, like a hat pulled down over it. In front of the house was a small lawn, bisected by a narrow concrete walk, and in back were another lawn, a small garden, and a garage, which was reached by an alley that ran parallel to the street behind all the houses on the block. Facing the street were the front door and a picture window, and above each was a green aluminum awning, with a white stripe on the fringe. A cedar tree stood, sentry-like, next to the door, a box-shaped shrub grew under the picture window, and a white lantern stood on a man-high post that was planted next to the concrete walk. Up and down the street for as far as the eye could see were more such houses on small lots. Milwaukee is, by and large, a city of family-owned houses. Its streets, which are laid out in a strict grid pattern, run for miles in straight lines, and the house numbers mount quickly into the thousands as one drives north or west. Except in the city's downtown—about seven miles as the crow flies from the Gapolinskys' house—where glass-and-steel towers have risen in and around a remarkably handsome and well-preserved core of nineteenth-century urban buildings, tall buildings are rare in Milwaukee. The city's neighborhoods combine features of urban and suburban life. As in many cities, the streets are laid out in numbered blocks intersected by named avenues and a few throughways. Yet, as in the suburbs, commercial and residential areas have become separated as shopping malls have taken over from local stores, and workers have taken to travelling to their jobs by car. In general, people get from one place to another by automobile. No commercial establishment—neither office nor store—was visible from the Gapolinskys' house; they and their neighbors did most of their shopping in a mall about a mile away. Except when people were leaving for work or returning home, the streets were quiet and empty. When I pulled up in front of the Gapolinskys' house, at about five o'clock, no person or moving car was in sight, the living-room windows of most of the houses on the street were lit, usually behind drawn shades, and in many windows the cool light of television sets flickered. When I got out of the car, the sky—its low, slow-moving clouds underlit a dull orange—was a strong presence.

Bill Gapolinsky greeted me at the door, in brown slacks and a T-shirt decorated with a picture of an overflowing stein of beer and, below it, the word "BEER." Bill, who was twenty-six, was a tall, physically powerful man who carried himself somewhat rigidly, as if to hold his energy in check.

He had stiff brown hair, parted in the center, small brown eyes, a ski-jump nose, a brown mustache, and a broad, strong mouth. When he smiled, his eyes lit up with a mischievous glint, and a broken front tooth gave him a roguish, piratical air. But when the smile faded the glint was extinguished, and the pirate vanished, and in his place stood a sober, opaque, impassive citizen. Bill showed me into the living room. A plaid-upholstered sofa under the picture window faced two stuffed chairs against the opposite wall, and a nineteen-inch television set stood against a side wall. Above it were two pictures—a glossy photograph of a mountain scene laminated into a thin-sliced cross-section of a log, and a glassed-in photograph of a sunset over an ocean, in whose lower right-hand corner were the hands of an operating clock. A family of butterflies in a pattern of rising flight was fixed to the wall over one of the chairs. Framed photographs of Gina and the Gapolinskys' two children, Marjorie, four, and Linda, a year and a half, hung next to the picture window. The sound of children's voices and of water running floated down from the second floor, where the family's three bedrooms were. Bill said that Gina was getting the children ready for bed, and that all three would be down soon. We sat down to wait, and I asked Bill to tell me something about his work.

Two months earlier, he said, he had been promoted from salesman at the Standard American Cookie Company (as I'll call it), which sells cookies and other snack foods all over the country, to district manager for sales—an advance in the corporate hierarchy that formally elevated him from the ranks of the workers to management, requiring that he resign from his union. He had got the salesman's job, he said, only two and a half years before that, in February of 1982. With the change in rank came a change in his working uniform: as a salesman, Bill could leave his shirt collar open on the job (company policy discouraged this, but few people paid any attention); now he was required to wear not only a

shirt and tie but a sports jacket or a suit. Bill and a brother of
his were the first members of his family, he said, to rise to a
managerial position. Bill and Gina were both graduates of
the University of Wisconsin; neither his nor Gina's parents
or grandparents had gone to college. All four of Bill's grandparents had emigrated to the United States from Poland at
the beginning of this century. All were Catholic, and so were
their children, and Bill himself. All four of Gina's grandparents had emigrated from Sicily, also around the beginning
of the century, and they, too, had all been Catholic, as were
their children and Gina. Bill's father, who died in November
of 1976, worked for thirty years as a shipping clerk on the
night shift at the Pabst Brewing Company. Because Bill had
risen into management, he was covered for the first time in
his life by a dental plan that would pay to have his front
tooth capped, and he intended, he told me, to have this work
done soon.

There was a sound of laughter on the stairs, and Gina
appeared, smiling, with Linda in her arms. Gina was short,
full-figured, vivacious, and pretty. She had dark brown hair
down to her shoulders, large brown eyes, and soft, rounded
features, and she was wearing bluejeans and a lemon-
colored jersey with a cowl collar. Her smile was broad and
her gaze direct, and she conveyed a feeling of warmth, force-
fulness, and fun. She handed Linda over to Bill. Linda,
who was wearing red one-piece pajamas, had dark curly hair
and a willful twinkle in her eye.

"Here's our bundle of joy," Bill boomed. "I haven't
seen you all day." He kissed her noisily.

A few moments later, Marjorie came downstairs, wearing a flowered nightgown. She had long dark-brown hair,
delicate features, and a tentative smile.

"Hey, I missed you, sweetheart," Bill said to Marjorie.
"Do you love Daddy? Give Daddy a kiss."

Marjorie hung back.

"*Mar-jo-rie. Give Dad-dy a kiss*," Bill said again, with

menacing emphasis on each syllable, but Marjorie did not move.

"She doesn't have to kiss you if she doesn't want to," Gina interjected.

"You don't think so?" Bill answered, only half joking, and he made an abrupt move toward Marjorie, who started to flee upstairs. Bill followed, and shortly a happy shriek was heard from the top of the stairs, followed by loud kissing sounds and giggles.

"Why do I spank you?" Bill asked, still out of sight at the top of the stairs.

"Because you love me," Marjorie answered. Bill sometimes spoke in a commanding, aggressive tone, but often he would suddenly drop that tone and become docile and reasonable. Bill loved to be reasonable, and he was proud of his ability to listen to other points of view, and to let his own view be changed by them. But even when Bill was commanding, Gina was not overawed. She summoned a commanding voice of her own for these occasions, and talked back. She was also capable of making a public scene, and Bill knew this. On their first date, at the movies, they both recalled with amusement, they had had an argument about some Jujubes that Bill proposed to buy for Gina. He started to buy a four-ounce package from the concession, for fifty cents, but Gina noticed that a one-ounce package was available for ten cents from a vending machine, and she insisted that Bill exchange the two quarters he had for five dimes and get five one-ounce packages from the machine, and he did. Oh, boy, he had thought at the time. I'm arguing with this woman on our first date. This is probably the one I'll wind up marrying. Bill and Gina both were strong personalities, but neither showed the slightest sign of being intimidated by the other.

After Gina had put the children to bed, Bill, Gina, and I sat down to discuss the election. I asked Bill how things looked to him at this point.

"I'm leaning to Reagan," he told me. "I'm an optimistic American, and I think America should be able to solve problems. I'm kind of like J.R. Ewing, in 'Dallas.' " He paused. "Maybe I'm a kind of a jerk," he added diffidently.

Gina laughed. Her laugh was explosive; it came up from the depths and rocked her whole frame. "He thinks he's Mr. Executive now," she burst out merrily. "He thinks that if he votes for the Democrat he'll be brought down to blue-collar level."

"Sure," Bill answered, smiling, yet with a competitive glint in narrowed eyes. "But I have to go out and deal with reality and provide for the family. You're just a housewife, and you can stay home in the little warm cocoon of the house all day."

Gina's laugh erupted again. "Oh, ho!" she exclaimed. " 'Just'? Did I hear 'just'? I guess you think I'm sitting around here all day watching TV and taking naps."

"No, honey—honest, I don't," Bill said, his voice now soft. "I really think being a housewife is the hardest job there is. I know I couldn't do it. No way." Bill spoke with evident conviction. A sort of harsh kidding was one of Bill's styles with his friends and relatives, and sometimes he carried it to the edge of insult. For instance, he might repeatedly say to a guest, "Are you still here? I thought you'd gone." But before offense was given he would dissolve the joke in affection and hospitality. He enjoyed similar kidding from others, and never took offense. He carried no chip on his shoulder, and in his aggressive banter nothing serious seemed threatened against others or to be at stake for him. Since his promotion at Standard American, I learned later, Bill had been working as much as ten or twelve hours a day. But when he was home he shared the household tasks with Gina—washing dishes and clothes, changing diapers, putting the children to bed. Neither Bill nor Gina, they said, wanted the kind of marriage, common in their parents' generation but much rarer today, in which the husband came home from work, sat down in his favorite armchair, turned on the TV, and was served a cup of coffee or a beer by his wife. Bill admitted that the idea of being served that way sometimes appealed to him, but he said he had decided that the sort of woman who would offer to do it would not be interesting to him. He wanted someone more "challenging," he said, and in Gina he had found her. Gina now did part-time free-lance work as an interviewer for market-research projects, and she and Bill took it for granted that when both children were in school she would get a regular job.

I asked Gina whom she preferred in the election.

"*Definitely* Mondale," she said. "I guess I'm just a social-welfare-type person."

"Anyway," Bill said, resuming his train of thought about the election, "Reagan's selling himself, and I think it's working. He really knows how to get things across to people. He presents himself well. Even when he doesn't *say* something, you *know* what he's thinking. I think he's really a strong leader."

"You say he sells himself well to people," I said. "But does he sell himself well to you? And do you like what it is that he is selling?"

"I do like several things that he's done," Bill answered. "One, he brought down inflation. Two, he brought down interest rates from the twenty percent where they were under Carter. There's no way we could have bought this house with interest rates at twenty percent." Bill and Gina bought their house in January of 1984, for $49,000. They paid only $200 down and got a mortgage for the rest, at 12.5 percent, obligating them to monthly payments of $656.

"What he says goes," Gina observed. "Mondale is kind of lukewarm—like he was more of a team player."

"In the sixties and the seventies, it seemed like nothing the country wanted to do ever got done," Bill went on. "We wanted inflation to go down, but it didn't. We wanted American imperialism to stop, but it still went on. What with the

Vietnam War, and non-trust in the government, and burning the flag, there was a feeling of 'Why vote? It doesn't matter. Everybody's crooked.' But now it seems that people think that the government *can* do some good things. Reagan had a majority in only one house of Congress, but he talked to the people he had to talk to, and got his program through. Carter had Democratic majorities in both houses and couldn't do zilch. Maybe I feel like I do because of the other Presidents I've known. What did Nixon do? He made friends with China. Ford didn't have time. Carter was a washout. So when I see someone accomplish *anything* I'm impressed. I'm feeling better about the whole country. You know, around the time of the last election I was wondering whether we would all be here four years from now."

"What made you wonder that?" I asked.

"Well, you know, the hydrogen bomb and all," Bill answered, in a low voice, as if embarrassed. "And I didn't know whether I would even have a job or a family. But now I have all of that. I used to think maybe we all had a twenty-percent chance of making it. Now I think it's more like eighty percent. But I recently met a Jehovah's Witness who said it looks like the world could end any day now. It's still as if there's too much chance for something to go wrong. People talk about putting money away for the future, but—hey—I don't. I would *love* to be here when I'm sixty-five or eighty-five, or a hundred, and with Gina, too, and have Marjorie be a grandmother. But I'm not going to put a lot of money away which would prevent me from enjoying something right now, just so I could enjoy something when I'm sixty-five. I'm not totally convinced I'm going to be here when I'm sixty-five."

"In coming to feel somewhat more optimistic, do you think that the world has changed or that your views have changed?" I asked.

"My views have changed based on the world changing," he said. "Reagan put his foot down and said, 'This is what we're going to do, and this is what we're not going to do.' I remember once, when I was a junior in college and Carter was President, I went with my cousin Karen to hear this Indian folk singer, who talked about how we're 'wasting the good of the land' and how there's no way we're going to 'see twenty more winters.' And I really believed that. I remember asking Karen, 'Do you think we're going to be around in twenty years?' And she said, 'Oh, hell, yeah.' And I said, 'God, I'm really looking forward to having kids, and raising them, and waiting for them to have kids. I want them to go through everything I'm going through, and I want them to enjoy it. But I have the feeling they aren't going to be around.' "

"Do you remember what made you feel this way?" I asked.

"Well, it seemed there wasn't going to be enough oil, the way we were using it," Bill said. "And in London, I read, people were dying of pollution. And in Los Angeles the pollution was getting worse and worse, too. And all the nuclear crap was going on. It seemed like the whole world was closing in on us. Also, it seemed like the environmentalists and the draft-card burners were taking over. And especially the anti-Vietnam, anti-defense protesters. If we cut and cut and cut defense spending, I thought, then pretty soon we aren't going to have any weapons. Once we stop building weapons—once sixty to eighty percent of the people believe that you don't need weapons, when we reduce to that point —then what do you think is going to happen? The Russians are going to jump on us, that's what."

I asked Bill what he thought about Mondale.

"I don't exactly disagree with him," Bill said. "In fact, if he could do everything that he says he would do, I'd vote for him right away. But I just don't think he can. Take his idea of raising taxes, for instance." Bill was referring to Mondale's promise to raise taxes to help reduce the budget deficit. "I think it's a good idea. He wants the rich people to pay more. But they won't. They never have, and they never will. Mondale is just not going to be able to do it. There's no way."

"Why not?" I asked.

"It's just never been done," Bill answered with finality. "A lot of politicians are in office because the rich people put them there. The politicians owe them too many favors to make them pay higher taxes. Money just runs this country. God, I'm convinced of that. If there was no monetary influence or business influence, I'd definitely vote for Mondale. It's too bad, because I agree with him. But I just don't think he can do what he wants to do. He can't do it."

"Why can Reagan get things done?"

"He's more of a realist. He's a Republican, a business-man—he believes in business." Bill thought for a few moments. "So do I," he went on. "Partly because business makes America work and partly because you can't get away from its influence. You can't beat big business. You can't beat big money. I'm a conservative."

"Bill, I think you're beginning to sound a little *pessimistic,*" Gina remarked. "I thought you were supposed to be this optimistic American."

"I *am* optimistic," Bill said.

"You don't like the idea of being pegged as pessimistic, but lots of your ideas *are* pessimistic," Gina said. "You know, this thing like 'Sure, Mondale's plan sounds good, but it can never be done, because of the way the world is, so it just won't be put into effect, because you just can't do it.' And without even giving it a try. I think you just want to maintain the status quo by keeping the Republicans in there —because you're a little selfish, a little afraid you may get hurt." She added wistfully, "Bill, you've become so business-minded."

"Maybe," Bill answered, entertaining the thought. "You know," he continued, "at one of the Catholic high schools that I sell cookies to I saw a sign that said, 'Even if you come in first, act as if you came in last.' I think that's un-American. If you think in an uncompetitive way, you're not going to succeed in America." He stopped. Then, as if remembering something, he said, in a quieter voice, "You know, I really believe in pacifism, though. I really do. I was always good at sports—baseball, football, everything. But if people were hitting each other or hurting each other, I just never wanted to have anything to do with it. To me, it was just a game. It *could* be done in a fair way. I like to think that there are few people fairer and more honest than me."

"That's *true!*" Gina exclaimed immediately, brought forward in her chair with the force of the realization. "He *is* fair. He really is."

"Now, at my salesman job we were authorized to give a ten-percent reduction on cookies to schools, to bring in business. But some guys cheated and found a way of giving twenty percent without the main office finding out. That way, their records and commissions improved. But I just wouldn't do it. No way. Maybe my boss even wanted me to. He's a very straight guy, but maybe, although he wouldn't say, 'Do it,' he wanted me to do it anyway. But I wouldn't. One of my colleagues says, 'That's what's fun about business —breaking the rules.' But that's what I *hate* about business —when it gets dishonest."

"In your experience, are most people you deal with honest?" I asked.

"Everyone wants a break for himself," Bill said. "That's America. That's capitalism. That's competition. I think that one of the Catholic high schools I was selling cookies to took the account away from me and gave it to another guy because he offered the twenty-percent discount."

As Gina heard this, a troubled look came over her face. "But Bill," she asked, "isn't that the time to break the rule? I mean, isn't that what you have to do, ultimately?"

"So what *is* the ultimate thing, Gina?"

"Isn't it to break the rule? Isn't that it? Isn't that what Standard American really wants?"

"Yeah, sure it is," Bill answered. "But I'm not Standard American. I'm Bill Gapolinsky."

THE COMMENTATORS WERE talking about nuclear-arms control, the budget deficit, and other issues of the day, and Bill and Gina were concerned with these things, too, but as I talked to them it seemed to me that what divided them politically as much as anything was the question of how bad the world was—how unreformably, irredeemably bad. For Bill, the world—meaning, roughly, the upper reaches of power and money, where the politicians made their decisions and the businessmen made their deals—was a place where corruption was endemic, or, at any rate, more widespread than it was in the private spheres of most people's lives. But because the corruption was inexpungeably ingrained in the world it in a way lost the character of corruption and became necessary, and therefore even desirable. Certainly you didn't want as your representative in this harsh realm someone who indulged himself in inappropriate, private virtues—virtues whose only effect was to put him and you at a competitive disadvantage. And yet when Bill contemplated moving up into that harsh realm himself, as a businessman, part of him held back—nothing less than the part he proudly called Bill Gapolinsky. To be "conservative" did not mean that he thought it was a good idea that big money ruled society; it meant that he believed this to be the case, and thought that there was nothing to be done about it. Gina agreed that big money ruled society, but she hoped that this state of affairs could be changed, and wanted to put up a fight against it. She believed that acceptance of the rule of big money was not wisdom or realism but apathy, or even selfishness. Bill saw the world as in its nature quite bad; Gina saw it as improvable. Neither of the political parties was taking a position on how intrinsically good or bad the world was, but Bill's dark, fatalistic view of the world somehow was inclining him toward the "confident," "optimistic" Republicans and Gina's comparatively brighter view was inclining her toward the "defeatist," "pessimistic" Democrats.

A MAP REPRESENTING THE world of Bill and Gina Gapolinsky would have on it very few places outside Milwaukee. Two key points on the map would be the homes of Bill's mother, Barbara Gapolinsky, and Gina's mother, Martha Bellacchio, both of whom lived alone, in retirement. Mrs. Gapolinsky lived a few miles to the north of Bill and Gina's house, in the house in which Bill grew up, and Mrs. Bellacchio lived a few miles to the east of their house, in a rented apartment. Mrs. Gapolinsky, who was the sixth of nine children, was born in the suburb of South Milwaukee, where her father ran a hardware store. Bill's father, Thomas Gapolinsky, died of a heart attack when Bill was eighteen, and Gina's father, Richard Bellacchio, deserted the family in 1961, when Gina was eighteen months. His present home, in Baton Rouge, Louisiana, would be a dim point on Gina's map. He had returned a few times to Milwaukee—unexpectedly, as often as not—to see the children. Gina had not enjoyed those occasions. She resented what she felt was an assumption on his part that he should be treated as their father. She had no interest in further relations with him. Mrs. Bellacchio was the fifth of twelve children born to Pietro and Anna Giardini, in Springfield, Illinois. Pietro had held many jobs—railway worker, coal miner, and, briefly, bootlegger. Anna had raised the children and taken care of the house, which had two stories and six rooms. Her grandchildren, who spent happy vacations there, recalled a woman perpetually covered with flour standing behind a stove handing out invididual meat-balls on forks to swarms of children; they remembered her as "a saint." Barbara Gapolinsky and Martha Bellacchio had abundant time to keep a vigilant, critical, affectionate eye on their children and grandchildren, and the views they expressed over the phone and in person, censorious or otherwise, were the subject of many hours of lively conversation among their children.

The neighborhood in which Bill had grown up, and in which Mrs. Gapolinsky still lived, had changed since the family had moved there, in 1951. During the war, Barbara's husband-to-be, Thomas, had served in the Army, as a medic in Australia and New Guinea. After he returned, in 1945, he courted Barbara for a year, wooing her away from another man, to whom she had been unofficially engaged, and they were married in July of 1946. In the next dozen years, they had four children: Paula, in 1949; Fred, in 1952; Katharine (Kate), in 1955; and Bill, in 1958. All over the United States, men back from the war were marrying, buying houses, often with the help of loans under the G.I. Bill of Rights, and having families. The Gapolinskys bought an unfinished house in an unfinished development on Thirtieth Street, for $10,900, of which they paid $3,000 down. (Thomas was eligible to take out a loan under the G.I. Bill but decided instead to obtain one from a bank that offered nearly the same interest rate.) While the house was under construction, they would stop by every Sunday to see how it was coming. All around them were the sights and sounds of building, and of other people moving into the development, most of whom were young couples, like them. Many of the husbands were veterans of the war, and Thomas discovered that a friend of his from the Army had bought a house on the same block. Soon the new neighbors were helping one another. As it happened, the builder of the Gapolinskys' house died just before it was finished, so Thomas, his brothers, his brothers-in-law, and several neighbors completed it themselves— framing and hanging doors, and doing other work. For Thomas, the task marked the beginning of what became a lifelong hobby of woodworking, at which he became expert.

The Gapolinskys were quickly caught up in the life of a thriving and growing neighborhood, which suddenly sprang into existence around them. Many of those moving in were Catholic, and a new Catholic church was built nearby, and a new parish established. Dozens of family activities were organized, by the church and other groups. A parochial school was founded. The neighborhood children came to be so numerous that the parochial school before long had to improvise new classrooms behind the chapel in the church. The Boy Scouts and the Girl Scouts flourished. There were spaghetti dinners and Friday fish fries (a Milwaukee tradition), organized by the church. For church festivals, Thomas made prizes in a woodworking shop in his basement. He became an usher at the church. The neighbors became friends, and took turns holding cookouts at their houses. The Gapolinsky family became engrossed in sports. Tickets for Green Bay Packers games went on sale in late summer and the children and their father took turns camping out in line for as long as five nights to get seats. Paula began to play golf, and she still played in 1984, and liked to watch golf tournaments on television—especially the Hawaiian Open. In the memories of all the Gapolinskys, their life as a family in their old neighborhood was a golden time. Those memories, which have already developed the aura of family legend, are inseparable from their memories of Thomas Gapolinsky, whom they remembered as intelligent, self-sacrificing, kindly, and loving, and held in reverence.

Bill's earliest memory is of being dressed up like a girl by his older sisters. When I spoke to his sisters recently, they recalled dressing him in dolls' clothes, draping pigtails over his head, walking him up and down the street, and calling him Jill. They also liked to play hospital, with him as their patient. Bill now saw himself as a self-confident person, and attributed this in part to being the "pampered baby" of the family. His sisters remembered him as energetic, intelligent, and outgoing, but they also remembered a careless streak. In the year after he got his driver's license, he had three car accidents. The entire Gapolinsky family—

with the possible exception of Fred—loved to talk. Mrs. Gapolinsky, in particular, was renowned in the family and outside it for her talkativeness. At the time I met Kate, she spoke at approximately twice the speed of most people, and Paula, too, poured out her words at a rapid clip, though in a quieter and less assertive way than Kate. In family lore, Paula was the well-behaved, "good" sister, and Kate the rebellious, "bad" one. Paula did as she was told; Kate argued or, more often, procrastinated. In the room they shared on the second story of the house, Paula's half was always tidy, Kate's a mess. Kate's fighting with her mother continued up to the moment of her marriage, for which Mrs. Gapolinsky demanded that Kate wear a girdle. Kate refused, and wore no girdle. Paula became expert in what then were considered feminine accomplishments: sewing, knitting, crocheting, needlepoint; Kate mastered none of these skills. Paula received the highest Girl Scout award available, called the Marian Award. Kate summed up the situation for me by saying, "She's perfect, but I'm nice." The sisters are now good friends. In spite of Kate's rebelliousness, and in spite of a policy of Barbara and Thomas's of treating all their children equally, the family were agreed that Kate had been Thomas's favorite. He had loved to read history books—especially those having to do with the Second World War—and Kate came to share his passion. Often, she would ask him about historical subjects, and he would tell her what he had learned from his reading. He and Kate also shared a passion for country music, and particularly for the music of the country singer Jim Reeves, whose albums they bought faithfully, and listened to together.

Thomas's sudden, unexpected, and greatly mourned death, in 1976, marked the end of the Gapolinskys' family life under the same roof. Within a year, the house was empty of children, and their mother was left there alone. Paula had left four months before Thomas's death, when she got married, and Bill left a month after Paula, when he had entered the University of Wisconsin. On that occasion, Thomas had looked into Barbara's eyes and said, "Now, Barbara, it's just going to be you and me, because our baby is gone." Six weeks after his father died, Fred enlisted in the Marines. An American flag had been placed in Thomas's casket, and the sight had filled Fred with overwhelming pride. It meant that his father, who had been strongly patriotic, had stood for something in his life, Fred felt, and he wanted a similar flag to be placed in his own casket when he died. Mourning and patriotism fused, and he made his decision to join the Marines, in which he served for three years. Now he lived in Oshkosh, Wisconsin, working as a manufacturing engineer for a company that made trucks. Fred's intense patriotism, his devotion to the military, and what Bill felt was sometimes an excessive, "macho" rigidity and emotional tightness had placed a distance between the two brothers for a while; now they were closer, and occasionally, Bill told me, they would go out and drink themselves under the table. Fred usually voted Republican, but he had voted for Jimmy Carter in 1976. This year, he favored Reagan. Bill attributed some of his own conservatism to the influence of Fred during his years of military service. While Bill was in college, Fred had suggested that Bill might enter the officer-training program, and then serve after graduation, but Gina, who has little taste for the military life, strenuously and successfully opposed this. Kate had been the last to leave the house. In 1977, she had got a job sorting mail at the Milwaukee main post office, and in September of 1977 she had married a chemical-company employee named Pete Lueders, who subsequently got a job at the post office. Now she was six months pregnant. She and Pete had decided that when the baby was born he would quit his job and stay home to take care of the baby and the house, while Kate continued working for the post office. Kate liked the work there but disliked housework; for Pete, it was the other way around.

The prospect that Kate would work while Pete stayed at

home taking care of the baby upset Mrs. Gapolinsky; in this and in other matters, she preferred conventional arrangements. Kate and Pete, however, felt that she was sometimes too much interested in appearances—in what the neighbors would say. But Pete pointed out to me that those neighbors could know of his and Kate's unorthodox decision only because Mrs. Gapolinsky, indulging her love of talking, had told them in the first place. Both Kate and Pete were strongly committed Democrats, for whom a vote for Mondale was all but a foregone conclusion. Paula's husband, Richard Mueller, had been married before, and had two children, who lived with their mother. He was not a Catholic, and Paula's choice of him had been a further jolt to Mrs. Gapolinsky's conventional hopes for her children's lives. Still another shock came along soon: the discovery that Bill had started to smoke marijuana in college. "My sophomore year was pretty much obliterated," Bill told me. Later, he quit. Both sisters had defended their unconventional decisions to their mother by pointing out to her that unconventional things were now going on all around her, including in her own neighborhood. They pointed out that not far from Mrs. Gapolinsky's house a forty-year-old woman was living with her twenty-five-year-old lover, and that the couple living right next door to her were not married, either. Mrs. Gapolinsky had disapproved of this arrangement, but had softened toward the couple after the man began doing odd jobs for her around the house. In several houses, the daughters observed, elderly couples had been obliged to welcome their grown children back after the children had been through divorces. And one of Mrs. Gapolinsky's own sisters was considering divorce, after thirty-five years of marriage.

Sometimes the daughters liked to try to ruffle their mother's composure by telling risqué stories. Paula—"perfect" Paula—once said to me, "I go over there and just start talking about sex. And Ma is like 'Oh, geez!' So, big deal, I think." Once, she and Richard told her mother about a time when they had had sex on a golf course. "We laughed so hard," Paula told me. "She was so shocked." It remains an open question, though, just how shocked their mother really was. Once, when Kate was dating Pete, her mother went away for the weekend, leaving Kate in the house alone. "Oh, boy, Pete can spend the night," Kate said to herself. "In those days, that's all you thought about," Kate told me. "At any rate, it's all I thought about." Her mother, however, forbade Kate to let Pete spend the night. He did anyway. Later, Kate heard something from a neighbor that surprised her greatly. Before her mother went away for the weekend, she had told the neighbor that because Kate was afraid to stay in the house alone Pete would be spending the night. "So while she was telling me not to let Pete stay over she was making excuses for me to the neighbors." Kate pointed out. "I was floored," she said, adding, "I think it's kind of neat." And when I talked to Mrs. Gapolinsky about some of the surprises that her children had provided for her she said, "You know, much as I want the children to do the right thing, I've learned over the years that if I try to correct them too much I'll become cut off from them. Then they won't even tell me what is happening to them. So sometimes I hold my peace. The most important thing in life, I think, is family, and I want to keep mine together."

For Paula, the closeness and warmth of the Gapolinsky family were thrown into relief by her husband's family, the Muellers, who rarely visited one another. Richard was estranged from his first wife and his two children. He rarely saw them or talked to them. They used post-office boxes as addresses, and he did not know exactly where they lived. (He and Paula have not had children.) His mother lived in Milwaukee, but in the eight years since he had married Paula they saw her infrequently. "She's very busy," Paula explained. "She plays bingo two nights a week, and sometimes more often." There were five brothers in the family, and they all lived in Milwaukee, but the last time they had all got together was when their father died, twenty years earlier. "They're all loners," Paula commented. When Richard attended the Gapolinsky family get-togethers, he was likely at some point to turn on a football game or some other program on television rather than stay in the conversation. His and Paula's life together had been marked by frequent changes. After leaving the military, he worked for three years as a food-service supervisor in a nursing home and then for eight years as a telephone repairman; then, knowing that he was going to be laid off, he took a job as a manager-trainee at a pizza chain. He and Paula had moved four times, twice because they had trouble with their mortgage payments. Nevertheless, they took annual vacations.

Richard's favorite vacation spot was Las Vegas, where he gambled, and they had been there six or seven times since their marriage. "It's great for me," Paula explained to me. "I can lie around the pool at the hotel all day doing nothing or I can shop. I have more friends in the Las Vegas Fashion Show Mall than almost anywhere else. The people in the stores remember me from year to year." Whatever the state of Richard's relations with her family, Paula was completely absorbed in him and devoted to him. During the day, when both of them were at work, she often missed him. A year before, when he was managing the pizza parlor, she had travelled at lunchtime to the place where he worked, secretly positioned herself across the street with a pair of binoculars, and watched him make pizzas. When I asked her why she had done this, she said she just liked the sight of her husband throwing the round pizza dough in the air and catching it on his fist. Paula professed little interest in politics, yet when I inquired what her views were it turned out that she was a convinced Democrat, and had never voted for a Republican.

Gina and Bill regarded Kate and Pete as the intellectuals of the family. "Kate is very cultural," Bill told me, and Gina said, "She and Pete read English literature and history and listen to classical music, and everything like that." However, Bill feared that Kate was becoming "too blue-collar"—that she was being too much influenced by the union she belonged to at the post office. He worried that she was "lowering herself by letting the sort of thing that unions complain about get to her." One example of a union complaint, he said, might be a demand that the mail sorters be permitted to sit in some particular way—back, rather than forward, for instance—as they punched the keys on their mail-sorting machines. "Kate and Pete don't get enough intellectual stimulation at work," Gina said. "It's almost like they're so lofty they can't apply their intellectualness. But if they get to a party, boy, can they show their stuff to advantage. Wow! They are *really* smart."

The old neighborhood had a friendliness, a liveliness, and a cohesiveness that some of the Gapolinsky children found lacking in their new ones. Kate and Pete were not well acquainted with even their immediate neighbors. Neither were Paula and Richard. During the day, many houses stood silent and empty. When Paula reflected on the differences between the old neighborhood and her new one, she was filled with melancholy. "Nothing remains the same," she said. "People are realizing now that those were the best of times. They'll never come back."

A few miles to the east of Bill and Gina's house was the three-story house in which Gina was brought up. It had belonged to one of Martha Bellacchio's father's relatives, who had become prosperous making custom-made boots—a craft he had learned as a boy from his father, in Sicily. He and his wife, who were childless, had taken a liking to Martha, and after she married Richard Bellacchio, in 1937, they invited the couple to live with them, in an apartment in their house. In the next eight years, Martha and Richard had three children: Louise, in 1939; Art, in 1942; and Harry, in 1945. Richard moved from job to job. For a while, he worked in a factory that made parking meters. Then he worked as a shoe salesman. Later, he became a part-time bartender. In 1959, Gina was born, and a year and a half afterward he left the family. "He married a whole string of women from here to Louisiana," Gina told me. During the first half of the century, the house was one of the most luxurious and well-to-do in Milwaukee, but by the time Gina was growing up there, it was in the middle of the city's expanding black ghetto.

Gina, born fourteen years after her brother Harry, had not shared a childhood with her brothers and her sister, and she saw them less often than Bill saw his brother and sisters, but when they did get together—on holidays, or sometimes just for dinner—the atmosphere was close and affectionate. Louise had contracted multiple sclerosis, and was confined to a wheelchair, in an apartment across the street from her mother's. Harry had married, had three sons, divorced, and remarried; he worked as a painter at Evinrude Motors. Art was married and had two sons, of whom one was about to go into the Air Force, and the other had just graduated from the University of Wisconsin; Art was the general manager for a Datsun dealer. In the absence of their father, Gina said, Art had become the patriarch of the family. Bill and Gina visited especially often with Art, who loved to cook, and lived in a house in an expensive new development a few miles north of the city limits. Bill described him as "a big-shot car dealer" who was friends with "some pretty rich people."

Next to their own neighborhood, their childhood neighborhoods, and the homes of their relatives, probably the most important place on any map of Gina and Bill's existence would be St. Paul's High School, which they had both attended. It was at St. Paul's, a parochial school, that political awareness dawned, if dimly. Gina did not recall that her family took any interest in politics whatever. "They were more interested in the fun side of life," she remembered. Bill recalled that his father was an unshakable Democrat, but said that politics were rarely discussed at their house, either. When Gina once asked her mother how she was voting, her mother answered, secretively, "I can't tell you." But on another occasion, when Gina asked her mother "what she was" politically, she had answered, "A Democrat, of course," and when Gina had asked why, she had said that the Democrats were for ordinary people like herself. And Bill remembered his father's saying, "The Republicans are for the rich, like the people who live on the East and West Coast, and the Democrats are for everyone else." Both Gina and Bill recalled that among their parents' friends—most of them working-class people—support for the Democrats, though not often mentioned, tended to be taken for granted. Bill entered St. Paul's in 1972, two years before President Nixon resigned from office, and three years before the end of the Vietnam War, and Gina was a year behind him. The wave of youthful rebellion that so noisily and visibly raced through American cultural and political life in the 1960s did not hit St. Paul's directly, but long after the restless news media had moved on to other preoccupations the social and cultural residues of the rebellion sifted down into the high school. However, by that time—the early and mid-1970s—the stereotypes that had been so vivid in the media (hippie, yippie, dropout, square, and so on) had blurred or assumed new meaning. For example, one of the cliques in Gina's class at St. Paul's was "the freaks," but its members were neither hippie dropouts from middle-class society nor the "effete corps of impudent snobs"—an educated élite in rebellion against the society that had extended them its privileges—whose political protest had so agitated Vice-President Spiro Agnew in the late sixties and had caused President Nixon to invoke a loyal "silent majority" of conventional people in support of his policies. They were, in fact, sons and daughters of factory workers, and, Gina told me, turned out in most cases to have been headed for factory jobs themselves. Neither academically successful nor politically aware, on the whole, they adopted only the style of

the "freaks" of media fame—wearing their hair long, sometimes with headbands, smoking a lot of marijuana, listening
to a lot of rock music (especially heavy metal), and adopting
a contemptuous attitude toward school and what it taught.
"They were just dirtballs," according to Gina. Since success
in school was one of the paths to economic advancement,
their rejection of it tended to ensure that they would remain
in the economic class into which they were born. (In Milwaukee as a whole, I noticed, as in other parts of the nation,
long hair, which was once associated with college students,
had slipped down a notch in the economic scale, and was
now to be seen almost exclusively among blue-collar workers—gas-station attendants, construction workers, repair-
men, and so on. I remembered that some of the strongest
resistance to the youth movement of the sixties had come
from blue-collar parents, and I wondered whether they
might not have feared—correctly, as it turned out—that a
style of life that was a passing fad for privileged college
students might have more lasting consequences for their
sons and daughters.) Two other cliques at St. Paul's were
"the jocks" and the "smart," academically capable students,
and it was usually they, Gina had found, who moved upward
economically, into white-collar or professional jobs. Bill,
whom Gina referred to as having been "Mr. Collegiate" at
St. Paul's, was in the jock clique, and Gina drifted between
cliques.

Generally speaking, by the time the influence of the
youth movement made itself felt at St. Paul's its political
content had been left behind, and only its social and cultural
content—the rock music, the drugs, and a general loosening
of sexual and other restrictions—remained. A survey made
by a St. Paul's student paper in 1976 found that half of those
responding had experimented with drugs. Bill's sister Kate
remembered that when she learned that someone who
smoked as much marijuana as Bill did in his first years at
college was becoming politically conservative she had at

first been surprised. "You know, I thought, Dopehead: liberal," she told me. "But that wasn't the case anymore at all." Now she believed that drug use was not a good indicator of political opinion. Sexual prohibitions seemed to relax at St. Paul's in the early seventies, but by the time Gina graduated a reaction had set in. In a class above hers, she recalled, some of the students had gone to one girl's basement to play a game called Seven Minutes in Heaven, in which a couple were shut into a darkened room for seven minutes, with the idea that they could do whatever they liked with each other sexually while the others waited outside. In Gina's class, such wildness had halted, and the girls adopted a virginal, almost babyish style of behavior, which Gina described to me as "cutesy," and "goody two shoes." For example, they would bring one another lollipops with ribbons tied around the sticks, and send one another sentimental greeting cards or notes. Bill still had a letter written to him in the cutesy style by a girlfriend in his senior year. It read:

Dear my you
My you're very special, cuz no one's specialer as a you, than you. You & i are us no one else could ever make up an us, 'cept "us" i do love you forever
patti

"I guess we wanted to hold on to our childhoods a little longer—to be immature and innocent," Gina explained. "Our attitude supposedly was 'Necking in the back of a car —oh, ugh, how horrible!' " Later, though, she came to doubt whether the most proper-seeming, goody-two-shoes girls had been as proper as they made themselves out to be. "They were in the back seat of the car like everyone else— only more so," she surmised. "And drinking and dope certainly continued. I was heavy into dope—but only on Saturday, and never in school."

Large and important events of the first half of this century—the Depression, the Second World War—had left most of the blue-collar voters of Milwaukee with their strong, if often tacit, allegiance to the Democratic Party, but if the students at St. Paul's were any indication the parents had not passed this allegiance along to their children. Being unspoken, perhaps, it had gone unlearned. Yet neither did the most dramatic political events of their children's own lives so far—for example, the Vietnam War and the resignation of Richard Nixon after the Watergate disclosures—leave deep political marks. In fact, as Gina and Bill and other graduates of St. Paul's whom I talked to remembered it, there had been very little interest in politics at St. Paul's. The only sign of political concern that Gina and Bill could remember was that in 1976, Bill's senior year, when Gerald Ford and Jimmy Carter were running for President, there had been one student in the class, Bruce Franklin, who was an impassioned and active campaigner for Ford. From the fact that Franklin's activity was so notable and odd-seeming at the time, Gina and Bill now deduced that the political sentiment of the class had been tepid, taken-for-granted support of Carter, if only because he was the Democrat.

"Bruce thought Ford was the next George Washington," Bill recalled.

"He had a locker full of Republican campaign literature, and we thought he was weird," Gina said.

The Watergate crisis ended with the resignation of President Nixon in the summer of 1974, when Bill was about to enter his junior year and Gina her sophomore year, and the Vietnam War ended with the fall of Saigon in April of 1975, but neither event made a large impression on either of them. When I asked Gina whether she had taken an interest in the Watergate affair, she answered, "I have no memory of it. There were so many *names*. My body was changing rapidly. I was interested in interpersonal things. I was more concerned with whether I could find a sweater that matched my skirt than I was with anything political." When I asked what the level of her interest in the Vietnam War had been, she answered, "Pretty much the same." She did remember one thing about the war, however: napalm. "Burning up women and children with *that* stuff couldn't be right," she said to me. "I knew that much." Bill recalled that his interest in the Watergate crisis and the Vietnam War had been equally low. In talking to them about either of these things, I sensed that both events had sunk below the horizon of the past well before they began to think about politics. When I asked Bill what his feelings about Watergate were now, he said he thought that Nixon had been "a crook" of some kind. However, he thought that most politicians were no less corrupt than Nixon had been, and so did not hold Nixon's misbehavior against him. What he did hold against Nixon was that he had let himself be caught. Believing, as he did, that politicians often had no choice but to be corrupt, Bill wanted them at least to be competent in their corruption. That was part of their job. If they were incompetent in their corruption, and let themselves get caught, they deserved to be forced out of office, as Nixon had been. When I asked Bill whether he now believed that the Vietnam War had been a mistake, his answer was, "Just about everyone in the country had decided that it was a mistake"; and when I asked whether, disregarding the opinions of others, *he* thought that it had been a mistake, he answered that he didn't have enough information to judge, but that "we shouldn't have fought there if we didn't plan to win." But when I asked whether he meant that we should never have entered the war or that we should have persisted in it until we won he again answered that he would need more information to judge. He felt, however, that in any case the Reagan Administration had studied the Vietnam War and would avoid making a similar mistake. "They have calibrated things more carefully," he said.

In her senior year, Gina dated a boy named Jim Krauss, who had founded an unofficial student newspaper called

Speak-Easy. Krauss (whom I talked to later) remembered that on their first date he and Gina had gone to the Milwaukee lakefront, where they stopped at a local gun club, and then had gone back to Gina's house and baked cookies. The *Speak-Easy* logo was an American eagle holding a bottle of liquor in its talons, and its motto was "The ultimate newspaper." In a front-page article, Krauss described the editorial philosophy of his paper in these terms: "Unless an article can approach an event from a unique angle, it would be better left unwritten. That is why most *Speak-Easy* articles are either editorialistic or humorous—school news is bland." An article on the dean of students, a Mr. Nordberg, described him as a "domineering and even hard-nosed person," yet granted that he "is not harsh or insensitive to reason, nor does he close his mind to new ideas." In another issue, there was an article by Gina on the social-science teacher, Mr. Lytinsky, which was entirely favorable to its subject. Gina wrote of "Mr. Lyt" that "his understanding of yesterday, his help today, and his knowledgeable predictions for our tomorrows can be an invaluable resource to anyone with a personal or academic problem." Another article, called "You've Got to Change Your Evil Ways, Teachers," took some of the teachers to task for using bad language on occasion.

When I asked Krauss what the political atmosphere of the school had been, he answered, "Malleable." He offered his own behavior as an example. His political inclinations were left-leaning anti-establishment, yet in 1976, when he was a junior, and a friend invited him to do some work for the Reagan campaign, he agreed. He actually met Reagan, in a Milwaukee hotel. Krauss, too, remembered Bruce Franklin's zealotry for Gerald Ford. "Certainly no one was for Carter very strongly," he recalled. As for the turbulence of the sixties, it had been boiled down in people's minds, he thought, to a "kind of newsreel": "Here's marching in the streets; here is the Vietnam War; here are the Beatles; here's

JFK being shot—oops, sorry—and here is the concert at Woodstock." As for the Vietnam War, it had been "like catching your parents in bed having sex," Krauss said, explaining, "Something disturbing had happened, but no one was saying exactly what. Probably because of Vietnam, our teachers did not raise us to believe that the United States could do no wrong. But we weren't told that the United States had *done* something wrong, either." Instead of feeling mounting dismay as the Vietnam debacle led into the Watergate debacle, Krauss and his friends were conditioned by the first event not to be shocked by the second. In his opinion, the cynicism bred by Vietnam helped to explain the indifference to Watergate. " 'Nixon stole something' was the general impression," he said. "I think that the most important effect of Vietnam on our education was what we were *not* told: that the United States was an altruistic country that always did right, which is what kids used to be told in school. Not having been taught to expect much of our country or our leaders, we weren't disappointed when they turned out to be corrupt. We were not startled that a President should be forced from office for misconduct."

Bill's office, at the local headquarters of Standard American, was about twenty minutes' drive away, on the south side of the city, and his delivery routes had taken him, at one time or another, all over the city. No map of Gina's life would be complete without a few clothing stores—especially Gimbels, in a downtown shopping center. There were few things she liked better, she told me, than to go into a clothing store with a walletful of money and spend it. Until recently, Gina and Bill had dined out about once a week; since Bill had assumed his new responsibilities at Standard American, however, they went out much less. One favorite place was a local bar and dance place called Tomter's. Another was a combined restaurant, discothèque, and video arcade called Tom Foolery, on a main route leading out of town. For a while, Gina and Bill became mildly addicted to playing video games. They both particularly liked Ms. Pac Man.

At the heart of Gina and Bill's world was, of course, their own neighborhood, Sherman Park. It was a mixed neighborhood, and they enjoyed the variety. Immediately around them were a machine-shop foreman, a registered nurse, and a factory worker and his family. Up the block were, among others, a concert cellist, a mailman, and a woman executive whose husband was a cabinetmaker. Also up the block were Gina and Bill's best friends, Paul and Betty Toruncyk. He was a former seminarian who now worked for his father-in-law's oil company; she worked as a counsellor for children of parents who suffered from alcoholism and other forms of addiction. They had two children—a son, aged three, and a daughter, aged two—who played with the Gapolinskys' children. Other friends on the block included the mailman, Steve O'Rourke, and his wife, Wendy, who was a housewife; Eugene Dzundza, who worked in an auto factory, and his wife, Helen, who was a nurse; and Fred and Elizabeth Skoretsky, who both worked as occupational therapists for the handicapped, and were devoted Catholics and dedicated activists in the anti-abortion movement. They were known in the neighborhood—a predominantly Catholic one, with a fairly large Jewish minority—for their religious and political zeal, which also included opposition to nuclear weapons. On the back of their car was a bumper sticker that read "Ban the Bomb, Not the Baby." Bill and Gina were Catholics of a more relaxed sort; they attended church on and off, and planned to send their daughters to the local parochial school, but rarely discussed religious matters away from church.

Bill and Gina's neighborhood lacked the homogeneity and cohesiveness that Bill's old neighborhood had possessed; yet life on their block was lively, and in point of friendliness yielded nothing to the old neighborhood. If anything, just because the cast of characters on the block was diverse and was constantly changing, a greater effort was required, and made, to hold the community together. The young couples who formed most of Bill and Gina's acquaintance were largely newcomers, but they were sociable newcomers. They gathered often, in a spirit of hospitable, neighborly camaraderie—in a "women's group" (devoted mostly to the problems of child-raising and other family tasks), in block parties (a popular institution in Milwaukee), and for less formal activities of all kinds; there were showers, Tupperware parties, Halloween parties, Christmas parties. While Bill missed the homogeneity of his old neighborhood, he was proud of the diversity of the new one, and associated it with a broad-mindedness on his part of which he was also proud. One of his delivery routes had taken him into the black neighborhoods of the inner city, and he was pleased that he had been able to work harmoniously with people there. "I want black people around us," he said to me. "Maybe not all around with ninety percent in school with my daughter, but around. They're part of America, too." Once, when Gina suggested that his racial tolerance was mostly lip service, he protested vigorously. "When I'm on the job, and someone uses the word 'nigger,' then even if there are no black guys around I feel offended. Sometimes I'll say something like 'Hey, grow up, man, this is the nineteen-eighties.'" His tolerance extended to other minorities as well. Not far from the Gapolinskys, two homosexual men shared a house. "I give them as many free cookies from Standard American as anyone else," Bill told me. "They're real nice guys—friendly and normal-acting. Now, if they started kissing each other in the back yard, that would *turn my stomach*. But they don't do anything like that. I like them. I really do." Something about the Gapolinskys' life had led Gina's two brothers to refer to her as "our sister the Yuppie." When I asked Gina what that meant, she said that it meant that although she and Bill had enough money to move out to the suburbs, they had not done so. Both of them, she said, had decided that they preferred city living. "I get itchy if I see more than one tree on a lot," Gina said. Also Yuppie-ish, she added, was the fact that Bill was "very ambitious." When I asked what she thought being a Yuppie meant politically, she said that to Bill it meant being a business executive, and that meant Republican, and she agreed with him.

The Gapolinskys and others I spoke to expressed pleasure and pride in their neighborhood, but an undercurrent of anxiety was also evident. The Sherman Park neighborhood had been a battleground in a drama whose actors were not so much individual peple as impersonal forces—the drama, enacted in many American cities in the last few decades, in which a growing population of black people in the inner city expands into traditionally white neighborhoods, driving down real-estate values and precipitating white flight to the suburbs. It is a drama that has often been exacerbated by real-estate companies, which, since they get a commission on each sale of a house and have a financial interest in rapid turnover, may deliberately "steer" black customers into a particular white neighborhood, in the hope of panicking the white population and touching off a chain reaction of sales. Sherman Park differed from some other neighborhoods faced with steering and white flight in that it fought back. In 1971, a group of community activists, some of them veterans of the civil-rights movement, founded the Sherman Park Community Association, which proceeded to bring a lawsuit against real-estate companies for steering, an illegal activity. In 1981, the association won a court-approved settlement with the Wauwatosa Realty Company for $40,000. Later, the association brought a contempt-of-court motion against Wauwatosa for its alleged failure to abide by the terms of the settlement, but lost it.

The Gapolinskys and their neighbors now kept an eye on property values in the neighborhood, so that news of how much a house on the block sold for travelled fast. The amount of crime, much of it attributable to young black men, had risen. One night when the Gapolinskys returned from an evening out, they found that two pumpkins that they had put out in preparation for Halloween had been smashed. Recently, they heard that someone's house had been robbed. On many windows up and down the block were signs announcing participation in Block Watch—an association organized to report crime or the presence of suspicious-looking people in the neighborhood. There were few black residents on the Gapolinskys' street or on the streets immediately around theirs, but twenty blocks to the east most of the houses were owned by black people, and a majority of the people in the local shopping mall were black. Kate lived in a thoroughly integrated neighborhood, and an increasing number of black people were moving into Bill's old neighborhood, in which his mother still lived. Bill estimated that the price of an average house there had been falling by about a thousand dollars a year for the last five years or so, and he attributed the fall to the fears of "ignorant white prejudiced bigots." In general, Bill associated racial prejudice with lack of education and with economic unsuccess, and was glad that his own rise in the world had freed him from intolerance.

One place outside Milwaukee that loomed large (prospectively, at least) in Bill and Gina's world was "the tower"—the national headquarters of the Standard American Cookie Company, in Houston, where Bill was likely to find himself posted if he got another promotion or two. The thought aroused ambivalence in him. Promotion would mean the fulfillment of his ambition. But it would also take him and Gina away from Milwaukee—the known world for them so far—and that possibility filled both of them with profound uneasiness.

GINA TURNED THE Gapolinskys' blue Toyota Corolla east onto Capitol Drive—a broad avenue that runs nearly nine miles in a straight line from Lake Michigan, in the east, to the western boundary of the city. She and I were on our way to East Milwaukee, to visit the house in which she grew up. We passed factories, service stations, warehouses, homes, halfhearted shopping malls, storage lots, fast-food places, drive-in stores, and parking lots, among other things—a planless assortment of residences and commercial enterprises of a kind that is now often found in and outside of American cities but that none of the usual words, such as "urban" or "suburban," seem quite to evoke.

"I didn't know I wasn't black until I was seven years old," Gina told me. "Our neighborhood turned almost completely black several years before I was born. All my friends were black. A few blocks from our house, there was a Lutheran church whose congregation was mostly white, and I remember that when I saw them one day I was astonished to see so many white people. That's probably why I have absolutely no racial prejudice now."

We passed a sandwich-and-frozen-custard place called Pig 'N Whistle, which had a parking lot on three sides, and Gina exclaimed, "That's where I was first kissed, on a date, in the eighth grade! It was in the parking lot, and my mother was waiting in a car, with a bunch of my friends in the back seat. They were all watching. The guy couldn't figure out what to do with his nose, and he banged it really hard on my forehead. It was just such a poorly planned thing." She went on, "Bill and I were both at St. Paul's, but we didn't get involved until he was a freshman at college and I was getting ready to go there the next year. He asked me if he could 'help plan my curriculum.' Ha, ha, ha."

I asked how she had liked high school.

"It was wonderful," she said. "You know how in high school you want to compete to be popular. I was real into that. I did everything. I was a pom-pom girl: rah-rah, short skirt, jumping—all of those things. One of my biggest disappointments was when I wasn't made a pom-pom girl in my senior year. Boy, was that a crisis! I guess I always loved school—maybe because I had a sense of sadness about the fact that I didn't have a family to fall back on at home, since my brothers and sister had all grown up and left the house by then and my mother was out working and my father wasn't there. When I got home, no one was there. Mom didn't get home from work until seven o'clock. Sometimes I'd spend the afternoon at her sister's house. She became a sort of second mother to me."

I asked how she and Bill had got married.

"At college, Bill and I got heavily involved. I lived in a house with nine other women, and Bill stayed over a lot. We practically lived together." In those years, Gina recalled, the women in college were becoming more open and assertive sexually. As a joke, Gina's roommate, Kim, would sometimes crawl into bed for a moment with Gina and Bill. Once, when they were in bed, she stood on top of a bureau at the foot of the bed, yelled "Superma-a-a-n!" and leaped on top of them. It was around that time that Bill began to smoke marijuana, at the urging of Gina. Before that, he had told me, he considered it "immoral and socially degrading." Gina went on, "And then we discovered Marjorie. I remember going on the back of Bill's motorcycle to get a pregnancy test, and they had them on sale, two for the price of one. We wondered how on earth anybody could need two pregnancy tests at the same time. You know—'And this one's for my sister,' or something. We got married in January of 1980. Marjorie was born in July. We had as much fun at college with Marjorie as we had had before without her. Bill belonged to a fraternity, and all of the fraternity guys helped us take care of Marjorie, babysitting for us when we wanted to go out. His fraternity was the first one that had a month-old baby. One difference was that Bill's grades just shot up —from a two-point-three average to a three-point-five average. He knew he was working to meet a responsibility to a family. After college, we had a rough period. I worked for a while at the Milwaukee public defender's office. My job was to help clients write up mitigating circumstances in their cases. But that work burned me out fast. I learned from the experience that I didn't want to go into the field of criminal justice. Bill took a test at the post office for the job his sister had, sorting mail, and he got the very top grade in the test, but they weren't doing any hiring until '82. Meanwhile, he did odd jobs. He worked for a couple of landscaping outfits, raking leaves, mowing lawns, and plowing snow. For a while, he had a paper route, delivering *The New York Times*. I hated that—my husband the college graduate delivering papers. But then, in February of '82, he met a friend who told him that Standard American was looking for salesmen, and he got that job."

Linda was born in April of 1983, and they bought their house in January of 1984. Meanwhile, Gina had begun to do some free-lance work as an interviewer for market-research companies. Big changes in their lives, Gina observed—marriage, the birth of their first child, graduation, a job for Bill, the birth of their second child, buying their first house, Bill's promotion into management at his company—had come in rapid succession, leaving them a little dizzy. Financial and family worries pressed in on them. Gina was now worried, she said, that the fun, partying days of their youth, when all they had to do was "drink beer, smoke dope, and have sex" ("I'm exaggerating," she added, with a smile), were coming to a close and that the days of mortgage paying and bill paying, housework and job pressure were upon them. They found themselves in a tight web of interlocking pressures. Sometimes they considered having a third child, but that would cost money. One way of making more money would be for Gina to get a regular job, but if she did she couldn't be at home to care for the new child. Another way of making more money would be for Bill to seek further promotion, but then he would probably have to work even longer hours than he did now, and the whole family might have to leave Milwaukee for "the tower." Bill's salary at present was about $30,000 a year; he took home $750 every two weeks, and received about $2,000 in tax refunds. To this, Gina added a few thousand from her interviewing. The Gapolinskys found that even as things were now they were a few hundred dollars short at the end of each month. They made up the shortfall by means of quarterly bonuses and the annual tax refunds.

I asked Gina if she thought that the swift changes in their circumstances had affected Bill's political views.

"His parents were always Democratic," she said. "But he always inclined a little in the conservative direction. Also, he likes to get a rise out of people. He likes to twit the typical 'Reagan's going to blow up the world' blue-collar type."

"What type is that?"

"You know: the unthinking, down-the-line-union-supporting, uneducated, Democratic blue-collar worker. You see, sometimes Bill likes to be outrageous. His becoming a Mr. Executive Big Deal is kind of like a joke to us. It's so unbelievable. When he came home with his first Standard American business card, we looked at it and just giggled. I feel like he's trying to live out that role now. After Bill got his promotion, we went to visit a friend of ours who is a lawyer, and he said, 'O.K., you're moving up in the world. Have you got your Republican Party card yet?' We all laughed and laughed."

"How do you think your political views were formed?" I asked.

"Once, on the Phil Donahue show, I saw a group of women—Women Against War, or something—hold up a banner covered with dots that showed the number of nuclear weapons in the world," she answered. "It covered the whole stage. Then they pointed to just a *few* dots, and said, 'That's how much it takes to blow up the whole world.' So we have these bombs that can blow the world up a couple of hundred times, and we can't even create a hot-lunch program for school kids. Now, that doesn't make sense. I guess my ideas got fixed when I was growing up. We had civil-rights marches going on right in our front yard, and although I didn't understand them very well at the time, they influenced me a lot. Father Groppi led marches right down our street." Father James Groppi, a Catholic priest and civil-rights leader, led a movement in the 1960s to integrate all-white neighborhoods in Milwaukee, with emphasis on its largely blue-collar south side. "Once, around that time, people were shooting shotguns right in front of our house," Gina went on. "My mother—I can hardly believe this—was lying on the floor. The shots rang out. People were running down the street with torches and banners, singing. In the summer of 1967, the National Guard was brought in to restore order. There was a curfew, and I remember doing those little paint-by-number kits for a few days, because I couldn't leave the house. On the worst day, my brother Art drove in and took us out. The National Guard was in the streets, and they were beating people up. Art had a shotgun in the back of his car, and I lay down on the floor as we drove out. It was like the Second World War.

"After that, I really started questioning things. When I came into a room, conversations would suddenly stop. Then, I'd hear things like 'Those damn niggers, why can't they remain in their place?' But those are my *friends* they're talking about, I thought. What I mainly remember is that I couldn't understand what was going on. Later, in high school, I had a mulatto boyfriend—his father was black. My mom just wouldn't accept it, and I had several run-ins with her about it. It was real bad. One athletics coach always cut me when he saw me after that. Actually, though, I think my family influenced me to be tolerant, even though they weren't so tolerant of blacks. They were always thinking about other people. They were so generous and gracious to most people, and I didn't see why that didn't apply to blacks. Anyway, that's what I did. I don't know why. It was just right. I was pretty much taught to grow up nice and right morally. I remember one teacher in grade school who had a big influence on me. His name was Lawrence Kenny, and he's a county supervisor now. He had a way of dealing with kids—he liked to do the fun thing. I think he helped me understand what was happening in the civil-rights marches. I had nowhere to go after school, and I remember staying with him in the big, empty school. Then, when it began to get dark, I'd go home to the big, empty house."

We turned a corner, and Gina said, "This is the street." Stately three-story Victorian houses, adorned with porches, gables, towers, dormer windows, crenellations, and other architectural features of an earlier time, lined a street that was shaded by tall, spreading elms and chestnut trees. Everyone in sight on the sidewalks and in the yards was black, and most looked poor. Some of Milwaukee's least fortunate people, it seemed, had wound up in some of its most splendid dwellings. We pulled up in front of one particularly handsome house. It had three stories, a châteaulike round tower with a cupola, an upstairs porch, several chimneys, and an elaborately gabled roof. "That's it," Gina said, with a sigh. "It's like *Gone With the Wind*. It's such a beautiful house, and I loved growing up there."

There were no lights on in the house, but we spotted a young white man entering a similarly splendid three-story house on the corner of the block. Gina said that she recalled playing there with some of her young black friends. However, her mother had forbidden her to eat in their house, and had scolded her once after she accepted some fried chicken from the family. She remembered it as the most delicious fried chicken she had ever eaten. We asked if we could look inside, and the young man agreed, and gave us his card, which revealed him to be a developer of "classic" houses. He owned this house with a partner, he said, and was planning to renovate it and rent it out as apartments. "Adventurous" white people were starting to move back

into the neighborhood again, he said. More than once, he
used the words "Yuppies" and "gentrification." The interior
of the downstairs was done in intricately carved, dark-oak
panelling. Though it was true then that some of Milwaukee's
poorest people were living in its most beautiful houses, I
reflected, that situation might not last long.

WHEN THOMAS DONEGAN, who was the alderman representing the Sherman Park neighborhood in the Common Council, the city's legislative body, was getting his education, in
the sixties and early seventies, there was almost no form of
liberal-minded protest available to someone of his generation which he did not engage in. Born in 1945, in Chicago,
into a lower-middle-class family (his father was a salesman
for a wholesale electrical company), he moved to Milwaukee
when he was six years old and attended parochial grade
school and high school. In 1963, he entered the Jesuit College, in St. Bonifacius, Minnesota, where he began training
for the priesthood. In 1967, as part of his training, he was
sent to St. Louis University; there he began to have doubts
about becoming a priest, joined Students for a Democratic
Society, became active in protest against the Vietnam War,
and helped found a program to tutor poor children. When
Father Groppi made a trip to St. Louis to hold a rally to
protest racial discrimination, Donegan attended. In 1968, he
joined a group of students occupying the university administration building in support of demands for greater student
involvement in the decisions of the university. In the Presidential primaries of 1968, he worked for the campaign of
Robert Kennedy. And in the summer of 1970, after graduating from St. Louis, he worked for the congressional
campaign of Father Robert Drinan, in Watertown, Massa-
chusetts. In 1974, after graduating from New York University
Law School, he returned to Milwaukee. There he got married and had two children, and became involved in the fight

of the Sherman Park Community Association against racial steering. In April of 1984, he was elected alderman.

In early October, I met Donegan in his office in the spacious, ornate City Hall building in downtown Milwaukee. He had curly, sandy hair, and a short sandy mustache, and was wearing a blue shirt, a striped tie, and chino pants. Working at a second desk in his office was Terry Perry, a slender woman with shoulder-length graying black hair, who was his assistant. I asked Donegan to tell me something about the Sherman Park community.

"Sherman Park is probably the most interesting—the most diverse—neighborhood in the city," he said. He spoke with brisk authority, like an efficient tour guide. "It used to be a predominantly professional Catholic community, with many people of German extraction. Now many of those people remain, but it also contains the heart of the Orthodox Jewish community, who are concentrated mostly within a few blocks. They make up a very stable, intelligent voting population. They're concerned about the safety issue. Having founded their synagogues there, they are not as free to move as others are. Sherman Park has also come to contain the heart of the liberal white community. The Sherman Park Community Association was one of the earliest and most successful organizations of its kind in the city. It hasn't achieved true integration, though, in spite of its partial victories in the courts. The races do not do things together. The eastern part of the community is predominantly black, the western part is almost exclusively white. When a black mother and her children moved into the western part recently, you never heard so much talk. 'It's not that I'm against black people, but . . .' and so on. I grew up nearby, and back then it was solid upper middle class. Now it's a little farther down the social scale. I just moved back into the area. There are a lot of people there who are urban professionals—without being Yuppies—and who are committed to organizing and preserving neighborhoods. These are people who are not quite as committed to making bucks as some others are."

I asked how the effort to preserve the neighborhood was going.

"Is it working? It's a tough question," Donegan answered. "There are a lot of old-time Catholics who *want* to stay, but their Yuppie children are moving to the suburbs. People are just on edge. You know, there were some of us in my generation who really hoped that we could create a new society, a new age." Donegan had a faraway, sad look in his eyes. "But I have to admit that it's a *fact* that a fifty-year-old Irish Catholic wouldn't feel as comfortable in an integrated neighborhood as I would. Of course, the black couple may be just as angry as the white couple about crime, property taxes, and so on. Actually, the white and black communities have very similar interests on the local level."

I asked Donegan what he was hearing about the national election.

"A lot more people are voting Republican," he said, dispiritedly. "It might be something like sixty percent Democratic and forty percent Republican this year. When I was in college, we thought that through politics we could make life a hell of a lot more bearable—that we could create a better educational system, open up corporations to new people, stop unjust wars. But almost none of those goals were achieved. There was a lot of disillusionment, suffering, and pain. Our younger brothers and sisters were watching, and they saw that we didn't have the answers. One of my younger brothers is like that. He's not so much conservative as moving into *himself*. He sees no benefit in what his older brother is doing. More and more, I'm out of it. Or maybe it's just that the people in my age range are finding out from experience that it really does hurt to pay taxes. You hit forty and have a couple of kids and a mortgage, and you know once and for all that you're in the class that's writing the checks for what the government does. It can get depressing."

I asked if he saw any signs of a reverse trend.

"Well, the pendulum could swing," he said. "But what we seem to be getting now—in more ways than I can understand—is a reaction against the answer to social problems that the Democrats have been proposing all the way back to the New Deal: things like FHA-insured mortgages, Social Security, housing aid, welfare payments. We had been hoping that these measures would strengthen the social fabric —make it solid. They have been in place a long time; they were not taken apart—even in the Nixon years, for instance. Yet now we're finding that the social fabric is full of holes: crime is up, the housing stock is bad. People are now perhaps running to Reagan to find new answers, even if perhaps it makes them feel guilty. Maybe Reagan and Jack Kemp have an answer." He shrugged, and the shrug seemed almost to suggest that although he couldn't agree with Reagan and Kemp, and would fight them, they should have their chance.

"*That's* an interesting opinion," Terry Perry put in sardonically, evidently impatient with Donegan's saddened long-term philosophical talk of pendulums. She went on, with almost bitter intensity, "You hear things like that from constituents all the time. *I* find it *stunning, depressing,* and *inexplicable* that young people are voting for Reagan. For instance, one young Jewish professional guy I know is leaning toward Reagan, even though he considers himself a liberal. He moved back into the city so he could be near a synagogue. He doesn't trust the Democrats on economic issues anymore. He *wants* to believe in social programs but thinks, Well, maybe it's not charitable, but let's let the economy do its work, and anyway with Reagan in we won't have to pay higher taxes. And yet on most issues he disagrees with Reagan. He's worried about the nuclear issue, and he's worried that Reagan will appoint a right-wing Supreme

Court. As for me, I still cling to that old nineteen-sixties attitude. I've *got* to stick it out. I've got to keep on screaming. I've always wanted to be involved. I'm staying with my old views. I'm making everyone *endure* them, whether they feel like hearing them or not."

BILL AND GINA's best friends, Paul Toruncyk, the former seminarian, and his wife, Betty, who worked as a counsellor to children of addicted parents, moved into their house in 1982. Gina described them to me as "really *interesting* people," adding that if there was one thing she couldn't stand it was *superficial* people—the kind who liked to talk about nothing but food, and while eating one dinner would tell you what they had had for a previous one. The Toruncyks were "real seventies-type people," she said, and, when I asked what that was, answered, "You know—humanistic. People who care about other people rather than just money." She added, "Of course, they're used to having money. Her father owns the oil company that Paul now works for." After dropping out of the seminary and before taking the job at the oil company, Paul, too, had worked as a counsellor—to addicted adolescents, adults, and their families—and that job, Gina thought, had been closer to his true nature than his present one. "He's unhappy," she said. "The company job is not really Paul."

I met Paul and Betty one evening when the two couples went, at Paul's suggestion, to a lecture on "Christian Parenting in the '8os." The speaker was Dale Olen, a former Catholic priest who had left the priesthood and married a former nun and now lectured on the family to Catholic and other audiences, and he was speaking in a large, bare, fluorescent-lit, classroomlike room at the Archbishop Cousins Catholic Center, on the city's south side. The center had formerly been St. Francis De Sales Preparatory Seminary, and it had been there that Paul had been a seminarian. Olen was a tall, slender man of soap-opera handsomeness, with a quiet, soothing voice and an even, contained smile. He was dressed in soft shades of tan and gray—light-tan corduroy jacket, darker-tan knit tie, and light-gray slacks. An audience of forty or fifty listened with earnest, upturned faces. On a blackboard Olen wrote "How I Feel." His topic was how to deal with negative feelings in the family. As he talked, he often adopted the listener's "I" himself, saying, for example, "I have negative feelings," to mean "Let's say you have negative feelings."

He began by asking the audience, "What is the most satisfying thing in your life?"

Bill was the first to answer. "The feeling of love that I have when I'm hugging my wife or children," he said, in a hearty voice.

Gina was the next to answer. "The most satisfying thing in my life is when I see my daughters hug each other," she said.

Other, shorter answers in softer voices floated up from around the room: "Joy," "Peace," "My family," "Pride."

Olen went on to ask the audience to name some negative feelings—the real subject of his lecture—and, after hearing "depression," "anger," and "pain," among other things, said that people *should* have those feelings sometimes, that they were valid. His message was the need to accept one's feelings and emotions in family life, and only then—after accepting them—to attempt to deal with them. He drew a diagram of the inner life. It was a box, inside of which he drew curved lines, showing the emotions. Arrows pointing from without showed outside forces. Flexibility, he suggested, was one of the clearest signs of mental health, and rigidity one of the clearest signs of mental trouble. On the blackboard he wrote, "I Know What I Feel." He recommended that in order to preserve flexibility the family "play with change"—for example, by altering the seating arrangement at the dinner table.

During an intermission, an assistant informed the audience that members could buy tapes of Olen giving his advice, and suggested that if they played these tapes on tape recorders in their cars they would find them even more exciting than rock music.

At the end of the lecture, Olen invited written evaluations of his performance. Bill wrote, "It seemed to an extent that you were speaking to some undirected, underprivileged people of the nineteen-sixties. You stressed some very obvious things. I would like to see you instill interest rather than to sell interest. That makes you seem too much of a business. I did hear and learn some very worthwhile ideas."

Afterward, Bill told Gina, Paul, and Betty that he had been "turned off" by the sales pitch in the intermission. Paul said that in his opinion Bill's reservations represented a "typical Midwestern attitude," and that if Bill had spent more time on the two coasts of the United States he would be used to this sort of "slick, glamorous promotion."

At this, Gina cried out, "Oh, Paul, you're always pulling rank on us, culturally."

"Not on you, Gina," Paul answered.

Gina explained to me that Bill and Paul were highly competitive, and enjoyed kidding each other. Later in the evening, while they were discussing the visits back and forth of their children, Bill said to Paul, "We *take* your kids. You *get* our kids."

"I BELIEVE IN WHAT Olen said—that flexibility is the move toward maturity," Paul said to me when I visited him the next evening, in the living room of their house—a two-story brick- and stone-faced structure up the block from the Gapolinskys' house. On one wall was a picture of Christ wearing the crown of thorns, His face twisted in agony. Over a fireplace was a painting of jagged, stalagmitelike yellow peaks against a dark-brown background that might have been a desert at night or might have been the surface of the moon. Paul, who was wearing a tweed jacket, a blue button-down oxford-cloth shirt, and bluejeans, was over six feet tall, and had a large, round face fringed with slightly shaggy hair. His movements were languid, and there was melancholy in the back of his brown eyes. Betty was not yet home from work, and he was taking care of the children. "The seminary in the nineteen-sixties, where some of the ideas mentioned by Olen were developed, was a dynamic place," he continued. "After Vatican Two"—the Second Vatican Council, which met from 1962 to 1965—"the old order was passing away, but the new order wasn't there yet. For me, religion has always had an active component. My uncle, who was a priest and principal of St. Paul's High before Bill and Gina went there, was a very active and vigorous man. When I was seven years old, inspired by his example, I decided to become a priest. The political movements of the sixties—especially the civil-rights movement led by Father Groppi—had a strong impact on the seminary. My brother, who is now a book editor in Boston, had big fights about the war in Vietnam with my father, who was a lieutenant colonel in the National Guard. I was living at the seminary, so I didn't fight with my dad much. He fought in the South Pacific during the Second World War, and was very gung ho about the military. But at the same time, you know, I think he really hated war. He wanted us to win in Vietnam and get it over with. Politically, he was pretty independent.

"After leaving the seminary, I stayed active in the church. When Betty and I moved to this neighborhood, we found that we were in a pretty typical *Going My Way* parish. It may sound snobbish, but we didn't want to hear some Bing Crosby type lecturing us about family responsibility, so we started going to a quite activist-oriented parish called St. Agnes, in a neighborhood that is about sixty percent black and forty percent white. In the sixties, that neighborhood experienced a lot of white flight from the city, and a couple of activist priests decided to try to apply post—Vatican Two principles, and involve the community heavily in the church's work, trying to root the parish in the grass roots of the community rather than in the priesthood, and they did a really good job. But now the parish has been spending more money than it takes in. The parish school runs a big deficit each year, and I've been involved in a big pledge drive to improve the long-term finances of the parish. The present bishop is not very strong on keeping schools open if they are not financially viable. We're in a bind."

Paul went into the kitchen and started to prepare supper for the children.

"Can I get in your lap?" Gordon asked.

"No, me," said Therese.

"You guys!" Paul said. "You're really doing a lot of attention-getting." He gave each a turn on his lap.

I asked whom he favored in the Presidential election.

"I'm leaning toward Reagan," he said. "But I'm really indecisive about it."

"How have you proceeded from your life of social activism to considering a vote for a man as opposed to spending on social programs as President Reagan is?" I asked.

"Well, of course, I've now had the life experience of business," he answered musingly. "I've been around people who are constantly criticizing 'big government.' And then I've had some practical experience with government regulation. For instance, I've been putting together a new filling station, and I called the city to ask what permits I'd need. Of course, I'm new to all this. The guy I talked to said that they were going to run a test on the tank we were putting in, and that if it checked out we could proceed. But he failed to tell me that we'd need a different permit for the pumps we operated. So later, after I'd opened the station, a guy comes along and says, 'Where is your permit to install pumps? You have to pay six dollars per gas hose to the city.'

I had to make a special trip downtown to get the extra permit. It was an inconvenience and a total waste of time. So I can see how the attitude of the businessman becomes 'Get the government out, and keep your hands off our business, because we can do it all ourselves. Let the free market operate.' It's the first time I've had that perspective. And I can see the logic that follows from that point of view. So I find myself strangely and uncomfortably agreeing with what Reagan says. You know—I agree *if I work within that model.* Within that framework."

Paul was becoming steadily more animated. "And at the same time," he continued, "Mondale is beginning to sound like tired old liberalism to me. It goes nowhere. It just doesn't work." Paul hit the table with his palm for emphasis. "I'm not sure what the reasons are. I think that *ideally* his philosophy is nice but that . . . that . . ." Paul searched for his thought. "Well, it just doesn't work—whatever the reason. Maybe it's cultural bias—that people fight these ideas too much, or that they don't want to do these things, or that they are unwilling to change. It's just that—I don't know—I don't find Mondale talking about the real world anymore." Paul was speaking with strong conviction, as if borne along by the logic that followed from the political framework he had come into contact with at his father-in-law's business. But then a cloud passed over his features.

"Except on nuclear arms," he said, in a quieter voice. "Mondale is making more sense on that, which is an important issue for me. Reagan seems to have no understanding of the danger. I just don't like Reagan's insensitive bravado— this idea of just trampling on the sensibilities of foreigners, as if they had no right to *be,* just because they're not like us." Paul was now speaking in tones of strong conviction again.

"You mentioned 'tired old liberalism,'" I remarked. "But aren't some of the tenets of that tired old liberalism the very things that you have believed in most strongly and, in fact, lived by for more than a decade now?"

"I guess I'm not sure that I believe in those things anymore," he answered. "Mondale just sounds like Hubert Humphrey," he said, in a scornful tone. Then he added, "The welfare system needs reform."

The front door opened, and Betty came in. The children rushed into the hall to embrace her, and she took them up to bed.

" 'Tired old liberalism,' " Paul resumed, picking up the thread of his thought. "Yeah, I believe real strongly in the welfare system. I was formed politically by the Catholic social teaching, which talks about the dignity of work—the right to have a job. And I see the economic system grinding people down, especially in the last four years. The rich are getting richer and the poor are getting poorer. And there's a lot of pressure in the culture to get on board the gravy train. When I reflect on my life, I see that that's what I'm doing. I chose to jump on that train, to go for everything I could get." Paul looked despondent for a moment. Then he continued, "I have some seminary friends who are very left-wing—certainly socialist, if not Communist. We get into discussions about the way things should be—about the need for justice for the poor. A big catchword I hear is 'solidarity' with the poor. Now, I grew up in Whitefish Bay—a rich suburb, just north of the city, that some people call White Folks Bay, because it's sort of the essence of preppic culture. My parents lived on the poor side of the street, in a typical Milwaukee bungalow. So we were one of the poorer families in a well-off neighborhod. I saw a lot of nice things around me. I grew up envying kids who belonged to the tennis club, with parents who belonged to the golf club, because our family couldn't afford those things. I married a rich girl, O.K.? And, incidentally, two of my brothers also married wealthy, and my sister married a rich businessman. I grew up exposed to the wealthy side of life, and even though I didn't have any part in it, wealthy people became legitimate to me. They're people, too; they're human beings, just like the poor. So when I have some of these discussions with my radical friends, many of whom grew up in Cudahy, which is a working-class part of town, in union families, I can't stomach some of their radicalism—for instance, when they suggest that every businessman is the devil incarnate. I just can't believe that. I know that my father-in-law is just a wonderfully good man. He does more for the poor than almost anyone I know—he's incredibly generous with his charitable contributions."

Paul paused again. "But then I reflect on what business is," he continued, "and I see the whole exploitive side of it. For example, the way you really push to get your employees to do as much work as possible, in order to keep your overhead down and maximize your profits. It's exploitive. If one guy comes into the office with an account for five thousand dollars, and another guy comes in with an account for fifty thousand, my impulse is to treat them exactly the same. But in business you don't do that. You invite the fifty-thousand-dollar guy to lunch, and you let the five-thousand-dollar guy sit for a while in the waiting room." Paul shook his head in dismay. "I happen to work in a company held by a family, of which I'm lucky enough to be a member, by way of stocks and other things. But the employee who's not a member doesn't benefit in this way. He takes home his salary, and maybe he's happy and maybe he's not, but nobody really asks."

"Of the two candidates, Mondale is the one who looks as if he would spend more on social programs," I said. "Are you in favor of that?"

"At this point in history, I don't like it," he said. "Not because I'm against helping people but because of pressing financial problems. Say," he went on—an idea coming to him—"you know, in a way, the national situation parallels my personal situation. Now that I have a family of four, I face the financial problem of making that work. I was faced with a financial dilemma, and I took significant action. I made a break in my career, giving up something that I like more, and that was more in keeping with my beliefs, in order to make money. And maybe the country is doing that, too."

Betty came downstairs, and she and Paul and I moved into the living room. Betty was a slender, attractive young woman with a pale, girlish face framed by blond bangs and shoulder-length straight hair. She wore a tailored tweed jacket, an ivory blouse with a floppy bow at the neck, and a gray flannel skirt. I asked her whom she favored in the election.

"I think Reagan is going to win," she said. "I don't see Mondale as a real strong Democrat. Although I do feel that a lot of social programs have been cut too much, I'm not sure I want to see them back full force. I have never voted Republican before in my life. Never. I tend to be more of a liberal thinker. But the thing is—and this is what's really important to me now—the one thing that I am really strongly against is abortion. And I guess—sad to say—I'm just single-issuing the whole election. In the next term, three or four more appointments are going to be made to the Supreme Court, and I want them to be against abortion. To me, that's more important than who is in the White House. So I'll be voting for Reagan." She spoke placidly and slowly, with little emphasis, as if thinking aloud, and she paused often.

"Is the intensity of your feeling about abortion new?" I asked.

"It's a feeling that I've always had," she said. "I was told as a kid that there was nothing more important in life than people—than respect for human life. That you open your door for all. Just the fact that there is a question about when life starts makes me feel that we can't take the risk of taking a life in the womb. I think there's a life there as soon as there's energy there, so I think abortion is murder. You know, I've always tended to see both sides of things, and I've always wanted to see something really clearly, and feel really strongly about it, and I guess abortion is it."

I asked her how she thought she might have formed her political views.

"My father isn't politically liberal—he probably votes Republican—but it was always his belief that people are the most important thing. His rule is: Always be kind and loving to all people. He puts human beings at the top of the line. If he sees someone who is hurt, he takes steps to help him."

"He's sort of like God," Paul added. "You don't even need to ask for help."

"Dad was the great protector," Betty went on. "He could fix anything. In the small town of Kimberly, north of here in Wisconsin, where I grew up, our family was highly respected. I remember being put on a pedestal as a girl. I was a leader in my class. I was at the top of the class academically. I was also seen as a 'Holy Roller,' a 'do-gooder,' a 'religious fanatic.' I didn't drink or do anything that was wrong."

"She wore the strangest clothes then," Paul put in.

"Maybe because of the values I learned at home, I've done volunteer work at various times in my life. In high school, I worked with Indians in Canada, and then, at the invitation of a priest who was a friend of mine, I went and worked in the ghetto in Philadelphia. I went to St. Norbert College, in De Pere, and when I was a sophomore I went to Peru and lived with a Peruvian family and worked at an orphanage. It was certainly the most invaluable experience of my education. I saw a whole different culture, and dealt with real poverty for the first time. I grew up in the sixties, so my father's money was something I decided to rebel against. I tried to calculate what I needed to be happy. I made a commitment to living life simply."

"Do you think abortion should be illegal?" I asked.

"Yes," she answered.

"If it's equivalent to murder, should people go to jail for having abortions?"

"No, I don't think so. I guess what I don't want is our government giving money for it or promoting it. It's really a dilemma." Betty looked vexed. "I have friends who have had an abortion, and certainly they shouldn't go to jail. If someone chooses to do that, I'm not going to stand in judgment on them. But I don't want the government to support it." She looked even more vexed. "Gee, I'm going to have to think this whole thing through some more."

I asked whether she would vote for Mondale if it were not for the abortion issue.

"Yes," she answered. "Because I think it's true that the rich are getting richer and the poor are getting poorer. Also, I think we should start to get rid of nuclear arms, and see if the other side follows us. I remember that when Gordon was born I had this feeling of being vulnerable, and wondering, 'Oh, my God, what have I got him into?' I had this feeling that I really loved this child, and that he was going to go through so much pain. One of the things that were real clear to me was that he was going to have to deal with nuclear war. But in recent years my fear has sort of gone down."

"Why?" I asked.

"Well, because people have really started to speak out about it, and to demonstrate. But, on the other hand, if Reagan stays in, and continues to build nuclear weapons, and you have these people who are trained to use them, *then they're going to do it.* I don't know. Maybe I'm going to have to change my vote."

The hour was late, and the discussion drifted to some of the philosophical and religious aspects of nuclear war. Paul and Betty began to discuss the possible end of the world.

"You see, it's my view that the world will be remade," Paul said slowly. "It's not a question of . . ."

"The end?" Betty asked.

"Yeah," Paul said. "I mean, I'm not worried about that.

I mean, it's going to be the end of the world as we know it. But it's not going to be a 'The End' end. You know, it's going to be another step in evolution. Whatever that is. It doesn't necessarily remain in a physical sense."

"So how does it remain for you, Paul?" Betty asked.

"How does what remain?" Paul asked sleepily.

"If the world is blown up, how does it remain?"

"It doesn't," Paul said with a yawn. "It's blown up. Physically, but . . ."

"But spiritually it remains," Betty said. "I believe, anyway, that the energy, the spirit—that which is life, the thing that connects us with all living things, with everything that is alive—continues to evolve to a higher form. And I think that I believe in reincarnation, where when I die my spirit may come back as another person, and you continue to evolve, and become more human and Godlike." Betty spoke dreamily, in a sort of singsong, as if reciting. "I think that in the end what it is is continuing to grow in awareness. In peaceful, loving awareness. And I think that total awareness, and total connection, and total love is somehow the end product. There's a cycle. You know, in terms of Christ's death, and of a child's birth: through a mother's labor, a child is born."

"Yin and yang," Paul added softly.

ON SEPTEMBER 10, 1984, Mondale unveiled a plan to gradually reduce the federal budget deficit which called for moderating the growth of military spending, reduced social spending, and increased taxes. President Reagan sought to balance the budget with reductions in social spending alone while increasing military spending and lowering taxes. By taking the unpopular position that taxes should be raised, Mondale hoped to win credit for courage and honesty and to throw a spotlight on what he saw as the impossibility of Reagan's plan. Reagan simply ignored Mondale's challenge, and accused him of being a traditional Democrat, who wanted to raise everyone's taxes in order to spend more money. The only day on Mondale's calendar, Reagan said, was April 15. The press and television gave the Mondale plan wide coverage, and it seemed that Reagan might feel compelled to respond in detail. On September 11, however, Reagan announced that at the end of the month the Soviet Foreign Minister, Andrei Gromyko, would meet with him to discuss nuclear-arms negotiations, among other things. It would be Reagan's first meeting with any high-ranking Soviet official. Politically, the announcement was a double coup. It diverted the main spotlight of the news media's attention from the Mondale budget plan to the Gromyko visit, and at the same time it undercut one of the most serious charges that Mondale had been levelling against Reagan —that he was the only President in the nuclear age who had failed to achieve arms-control agreements with the Soviet Union.

In early October, I paid another visit to Gina and Bill. Gina had sat Bill down on a kitchen chair in the middle of the living room and was about to give him a haircut. He had a cold, and his eyes looked bleary. He had been spending especially long hours at work, he said, and had encountered his first disciplinary problem in his new job: a salesman who was not bringing in enough business, and, furthermore, was not properly servicing his accounts. "The guy is a real dink," Bill said. "He has an extremely poor work ethic. I know—I worked with him as a salesman."

I asked Gina and Bill what they thought of the Mondale plan for cutting the deficit, but they were not aware of it. They didn't get much chance to watch the evening news, Bill explained, because he was often still at work, and Gina was giving the children their supper and putting them to bed. They subscribed to the Milwaukee *Journal*, a newspaper with a national reputation for excellence, but did not find as much time as they would like to read it. Their only other subscription was to *Milwaukee Magazine,* which dealt with local stories and rarely covered national politics. Once, when he was in college, Bill said, he had had a subscription to *U.S. News & World Report,* and had found its articles admirably "short and to the point." Later, he had tried *Newsweek,* but had found its articles too long and detailed. A great deal of their political information, Gina explained, came from watching the major political events on television, such as the conventions and the debates. Bill, in particular, was looking forward to the debates between Reagan and Mondale—two in all, the first to be on October 7. "I wish there could be six of them," he said. "I'm leaning toward Reagan, but if Mondale gives me a good reason I could change my mind."

Bill took pride in his willingness to give a hearing to views opposed to his. When Gina, who planned to vote for Mondale, disagreed with him, he would sometimes say, "That's a good point." This open-mindedness appeared to be associated with the affable, good-natured side of Bill, which many of his relatives attested to. It was also associated with the Democratic beliefs with which he had been surrounded in his early years, for it was to these views that he now, as a self-described conservative, had to open, or re-open, his mind. His Republican beliefs, on the other hand, seemed to appeal to the mischievous, rivalrous side of his nature, as Gina had suggested to me. In the world in which he had grown up, to be Democratic was orthodox, and to be Republican was to be iconoclastic—independent-minded, not bound by received ideas. His belief that his conservative views were made necessary by an ineradicable harshness, even corruption, in the affairs of the world was also in keeping with his mischievous streak, and it was not without a certain pleasure that he debunked Gina's gentler vision of American life and its political possibilities.

I asked Bill if he remembered any events that had lured him away from the Democrats and toward the Republicans.

Two stood out in his mind, he said. One was an article in a newspaper he had read in college which pointed out that surveys had discovered that a large majority of the college graduates in the United States voted Republican. "This might not reflect well on me," he said with cool self-appraisal as Gina snipped at his sideburns, "but when I saw the results of the poll I felt a kind of pride. You know how the Republicans are viewed as really being kind of snobbish? Well, all my life I'd lived in a working-class neighborhood, and I'd come from a working-class family. When I saw that most college-educated people are Republican, it made me feel like 'I guess I'm part of that—like I'm a little more educated, a little better than the rest, like I'm a little above all those working-class high-school graduates.' And I think that maybe in this way I let myself fall into a snobbish way of looking at things." The other event was his difficulty in finding a job after graduating from college. One of the landscaping companies he had worked for had been owned by two brothers of a very conservative bent. They pointed out to him that even though he was a college graduate, he took whatever job was available, no matter how humble—raking leaves, delivering newspapers—in order to put food on the table for his new family. The people on welfare could do the same, the brothers said, and Bill could not help agreeing.

As I GOT TO KNOW the Gapolinskys and their neighbors, I was struck by the inclusive spirit of the social gatherings on their block. The block had a life to which everyone apparently belonged almost by right: to be a neighbor, it seemed, was enough to get one invited to the rounds of visits and parties. Yet in a neighborhood as close as this one there were bound to be social distinctions, and these had their political implications. The term "Yuppie"—usually interpreted as a rough acronym for "young urban professional"— had both a stated and an implied "up" in it, yet that upward path appeared to be forked. One path up—up to more money, and to everything that money could command—was, certainly, the corporate ladder, which both Bill and his close friend and neighbor Paul Toruncyk, somewhat to their surprise, found themselves climbing. It was clearly a Republican direction. When you took the first steps up it, no one jokingly asked you if you had now taken out your membership in the *Democratic* Party. Nor did Paul find that when he went to work for an oil company owned by his father-in-law his egalitarian, liberal ideas *gained* in appeal. Another upward path, however—one that had strong appeal for Gina —was the path leading to higher and higher "cultural rank," and one vehicle for propelling oneself to those heights, certainly, was education. Yet education was not the only vehicle. There was something enticing about Paul and Betty Toruncyk's life that was less easily identifiable—something about the brick and stone façade of their house, about their tweedy clothes, about the fact that Paul's brother was a book editor in Boston, about the melancholy look in Paul's eyes. This other upward path, which Paul, indulging his "humanistic" ideals, had followed until he changed his job, seemed to lead to what Gina called the "really interesting" people, who would never describe one dinner they had eaten while eating another, and to opportunities to refine and broaden one's knowledge and tastes. It might lead, too, to opportunities to lift oneself beyond purely material pleasures and devote oneself to society's unfortunates. (Curiously, self-denial could be a luxury.) And this path, in Gina's mind—and also, apparently, in Paul's—was a Democratic one. Taking the route of corporate promotion, on the other hand, might well mean associating with some of the "superficial" people—even in "the tower" itself. Best of all, perhaps, would be a career leading upward in both directions at the same time, but such a career was hard to find, as Paul had discovered when he felt forced for financial reasons to quit his job as a counsellor of addicts and take the oil-company job. He had switched from one of these paths to the other, and one apparent result was a wholesale reconsideration of his political views. He had the wrong views for his new life, it seemed, and was in the throes of attempting to find the right ones.

"MY GOSH, WE'RE so up to here in church activities that we can hardly find the time to do anything else," Elizabeth Skoretsky told me, in a pleasant, low-pitched voice, when I went to visit her and her husband, Fred, in the orderly, immaculate living room of their house, up the block from the Gapolinskys. A grandfather clock, its ticking audible in the quiet of the room, which was heavily carpeted, stood by the front window. It had been assembled from a kit by Fred, who makes and finishes furniture; and other pieces that he had worked on were placed about the house. Both Fred and Elizabeth were registered occupational therapists, who taught handicapped, convalescent, or otherwise incapacitated people basic skills, such as dressing and eating. Fred now worked for a local hospital; Elizabeth had quit a similar job in June of 1982, shortly before the birth of her first child. They now had two children, Bob, aged two, and Mary, aged six months. The Skoretskys were devoutly Catholic, and were active in Catholic political causes. (It was they who had fixed on their car the bumper sticker reading "Ban the Bomb, Not the Baby.") Elizabeth was on the board of directors of the Pregnancy Aftermath Helpline—a group founded by Feminists for Life of Wisconsin to give counsel to women who had lost babies, whether through abortion, placing them for adoption, or miscarriage. In January, Elizabeth had helped to present the recent bishops' pastoral letter "The Challenge of Peace: God's Promise and Our Response" in an adult-education program; the letter states that "we are the first generation since Genesis with the power to threaten the created order," and finds that "we live today, therefore, in the midst of a cosmic drama," in which we are called on to "continually say 'no' to the idea of nuclear war." She had worked, too, to bring to Milwaukee a national program called Children of War, which was sponsoring visits to American schools by teen-agers from countries experiencing war in one form or another. A contingent of Children of War was visiting the Skoretskys' parish that fall. I asked them about their jobs, and Elizabeth, who had long, brown hair and a fair, rosy complexion, told me that hers had been exhausting and frustrating but had been marked by "peaks" of satisfaction, one of which occurred when a teen-ager who had been diagnosed as autistic when she was a child and still avoided touching anyone or being touched by anyone walked up to her mother and hugged her. Elizabeth had felt a certain pressure from friends to continue in her career, but had resisted it. "Some women seem to be trying to prove something by staying in their careers the whole time," she said. "I thought, To heck with it. To *whom* am I trying to prove something? I'm not going to jump through hoops held out by others. This is *my* life." Fred, a wiry young man with a small face, who was wearing wire-rimmed glasses, listened quietly.

I asked whether Fred's salary alone was enough for them to live on.

"It works—because we *make* it work," he said. When President Reagan proposed heavy cuts in social programs early in his first term and Congress passed many of them, Elizabeth went on to tell me, the program that employed her had to adopt stricter guidelines, and Elizabeth had written a long letter of protest to the Administration. This year, however, she planned, she told me, to vote for the President's reelection. I asked why.

"The most important thing is the abortion issue," she said. "The pro-abortion people seem to think that there should be some kind of test for getting into life. They think you have no right to be born *if* you're going to be poor—

that's a kind of means test—of *if* you might have some congenital illness, or merely *if* the mother finds that for you to live is inconvenient for her at the moment. I reject that thinking. I believe that there should be no conditions placed on entering life. For me, human life is sacred, period."

"It's an emotional issue for me, too," Fred added. "I think the attitude now is 'Hey, if you've got a problem, get rid of it.' Instead of taking responsibility for your actions. Everybody talks about freedom, but with freedom comes responsibility."

I asked her what her feelings were about the other item on their bumper sticker—the "Ban the Bomb" half.

"I've thought about that for a long, long time," she said. "When I was a freshman at college, one of my friends said that she could not bring children into the world, because of the danger of nuclear war. And I really had to think hard to justify to myself bringing another person into the world under these conditions. When I was pregnant, I had dreams in which I heard the bomb was on the way. After my daughter Mary was born, I had a dream where I was putting on her snowsuit—trying to protect her, because a nuclear war was coming. Of course, I know that a snowsuit isn't going to protect anybody against nuclear war. But in the dream that was my idea, and I remember thinking with horror that I had nothing to put on over her eyes. You know, you can put a scarf over a kid's mouth and nose, but what about the eyes? I've talked with friends about starting Mothers Against the Bomb, or something like that. When you're pregnant, you feel responsibility and love for this child. You feel, 'Don't touch a hair on its head'—let alone incinerate it, or, worse, leave it half dead to suffer. When the bishops' pastoral letter came out, it made me think over a lot of things. How much solidarity do I feel with the children of Central America, I wondered. Do I really feel that we all belong to one human family? If I knew that the United States was going to be wiped out, would I want the Soviet Union wiped out in revenge?"

"How in the end did you justify having children?" I asked.

"My main thought was that I am a practicing Catholic, and I really believe that God is present in our lives and in our world. To me, He is real. He is *really alive*. I decided that it would be the supreme act of faithlessness to despair. We have it in our power to make the bombs, and we have it in our power to choose life without them."

"How have these thoughts and feelings affected your thinking about the current election?" I asked.

"It's hard to say," she answered. "Mondale isn't very clear about it. His running mate Ferraro talks against nuclear arms, but I think she voted for arms appropriations. But I am disturbed that Reagan hasn't achieved any arms control. Now he's saying we can negotiate. I just hope he's thinking about all this."

I asked her how she had voted in past elections.

"For Gerald Ford in '76 and for Reagan in '80. My family tended to vote Republican. I was born in Elmhurst, Illinois —my father is an electrical engineer—and the whole neighborhood was heavily Republican."

I asked Fred to tell me something about his upbringing, and he said he was born in Oak Creek, Wisconsin, into a working-class family; he had four brothers and one sister. His father worked as a maintenance man in a factory that manufactured cooling units, and his brothers now held blue-collar jobs—two were factory machinists; one, laid off from a factory that made hydraulic seating, tended bar; and one was a fireman—and his sister worked part time as a loan officer at a credit union. Fred, who attended the University of Wisconsin, where he met Elizabeth, was the only one of the six to graduate from college. After college, he entered on his career as an occupational therapist. He said that perhaps because of his working-class background—but also because of his strong opposition to the Vietnam War—his early political thinking assumed an anti-establishment, and even a socialist, bent. In 1968, while he was still a high-school student, he supported the Democratic-primary campaign of Senator Eugene McCarthy. In 1972, he voted for Senator George McGovern. In 1976, he voted for Peter Camejo, the candidate of the Socialist Workers Party. And in 1980, he voted for Barry Commoner, the candidate of the Citizens Party. I asked whom he favored this year.

"I'm going to vote for Reagan," he said. He spoke slowly and unemphatically, in a reedy voice.

"How did you make the transition from Peter Camejo, a left-wing revolutionary, to Ronald Reagan, a right-wing Republican?" I asked.

"I don't think my basic philosophy has really changed," he said. "I've always voted on the issues that were most important to me. I believe in nonviolence, in helping other people, in the common good, in socialism."

"Do you see President Reagan as a champion of these beliefs?" I asked.

"Well, I have a lot of ideology that is coincident with the socialists', but it's not *total*. For example, most socialists are for abortion, and I'm against it. For me, it's a civil-rights question. The unborn are the most helpless group in society. Having grown up in a family of factory workers, I relate to how people feel downtrodden and oppressed, how they get to feel like mere tools of production. I believe in the value of human life. I still have the same principles, but I guess I apply them a little differently. Maybe I'm strange."

"What about economic issues?" I asked.

"On those, there has been a change," he admitted. "I now think that supply-side economics is valid—*to some degree.*" Fred raised a cautionary forefinger to underscore the importance of this qualification. "Also, I agree with Reagan on some foreign-policy issues. I agreed with the invasion of Grenada. I think they really went in there and cleaned out the situation. I don't think we should impose democracy, but I also don't think we should let the Communists gain power. I don't know. Reagan leaves a lot to be desired. But he's done a pretty good job."

IN EARLY OCTOBER, the Milwaukee *Journal* ran a series of articles on the baby-boom generation, by Nina Bernstein. The results of a survey of Milwaukee-area residents taken by the *Journal*, one of the articles reported, showed that in sexual matters the baby-boom generation, defined as people from twenty-three to thirty-eight years old, was much more permissive than people over thirty-eight. For example, 61 percent of the younger group "approved" of "casual sex," whereas only 28 percent of the older group did; and 77 percent of the younger group approved of unmarried people living together, whereas only 39 percent of the older group did. The younger group, however, was more inclined to "support the U.S. going to war" in a variety of circumstances. For example, 64 percent of the younger group would support the United States in a war to "stop the spread of Communism," whereas only 55 percent of the older group would; and 60 percent of the younger group would support the United States in a war to "protect our economic interests," whereas only 55 percent of their elders would.

In the first installment in the series, part of which was devoted to politics, Nina Bernstein reported on an interview with a man named John Carlton, who had campaigned door to door for Senator McGovern as a college student, and now worked for a firm that "devises tax-sheltered pensions for wealthy doctors." Carlton found himself "confused and regretful," Bernstein reported. Although, owing to "biases" he had "picked up" from his job, he believed that "Reagan is good for business," he nevertheless felt "cheated." Alluding to the assassinations of John and Robert Kennedy, he told Bernstein, "I feel like my life would have been different if certain people hadn't died. Sometimes I'm in real conflict with myself on what I really feel. I'm still basically a liberal, and I believe in the civil-rights movement and the anti-war movement and the anti-nuclear movement. Maybe if all the people who feel the way I do stood up and said, 'O.K., that's enough of this nonsense,' someone would listen." Meanwhile, he planned to vote for Reagan.

IT WAS "TIRED OLD LIBERALISM," and tired liberals, too—or so things appeared in Sherman Park. Like so many political usages, the word "liberal" is not so much a definable concept or a political philosophy as a linguistic bin into which various elements, some of them more or less incompatible, have been thrown in different times and circumstances. The same could be said of the word "conservative." What makes these terms hard, ultimately, to avoid using (much as one might like to) is, perhaps, that even if the notions contained in them are not linked conceptually they are linked historically, forming a clump whose fortunes rise and fall more or less as a unit in the public mind. In its dominant sense in 1984, the clump represented by the word "liberal" might be said to include, among other things, the following political views and inclinations: skepticism regarding the use of force to bring about political results in other countries; anxiety about the possibility of nuclear war; support for government programs designed to relieve poverty and bring about racial equality; concern for the state of the environment; and mistrust of legal or other government intervention in private, or supposedly private, matters, including, above all, sexual matters. It would no doubt be possible through careful study to give a history of this meaning of the term: to describe how the skepticism regarding military intervention stemmed from the Vietnam War; how the mistrust of government intervention in private matters was tied to the loosening of sexual and other restrictions in society in the 1960s; how the belief in social programs to help the poor and redress social wrongs originated in the New Deal and was strengthened in the civil-rights movement; how all these views coalesced in a rebellion against the status quo within the Democratic Party which culminated in the Presidential campaign of George McGovern in 1972; how McGovern's opponent Richard Nixon gave the word a heavily pejorative twist and then, by winning in a landslide, burdened the word with the odium of political defeat, an association from which it had never recovered; how in the late seventies and the early eighties the "permissive" social content of the term was separated from its political content, so that a majority of young people found themselves simultaneously approving of casual sex and of a hawkish foreign policy, as the *Journal* survey revealed—a combination bound to surprise observers accustomed to the political patterns that had taken shape in the 1960s. But, whatever the exact sense, or content, of the word "liberal," and whatever its history, being a liberal in Sherman Park—where liberalism by any definition had a strong tradition—was hard going in 1984. Paul Toruncyk, Thomas Donegan (the alderman who represented Sherman Park in the city government), his assistant Terry Perry, Fred Skoretsky, and John Carlton all found it an effort to maintain liberal convictions, as if in the invisible recesses where opinions take shape and convictions receive their nourishment a current had reversed direction, so to be liberal was now to swim upstream rather than down. Only Gina Gapolinsky seemed untroubled in her liberal convictions. She was the only serene liberal I had met in Sherman Park.

Bill Gapolinsky, Paul Toruncyk, Tom Donegan, and others had an explanation for the waning fortunes of liberalism: economics. To Donegan, that meant that the formerly young had discovered who paid taxes. To Bill, it meant that he had discovered the ruthless ways of the "real" world, and made an adjustment. To Paul, it meant that he and the country were going through the same process of tightening their belts in the face of economic necessity. Of course, every generation passes from the stage in which it is taken care of by its parents to the stage in which it must make its own living, and the process has usually been a sobering one. For the 1960s generation, however, the requirement of making a living, and all the obligations and worries that went with it, seemed to have come as a particularly startling development, as if it had never occurred to the young people then that they would have to find a job and pay bills. Their economic innocence may help explain how in the late seventies and the eighties careerism and money itself—immemorial facts of human life—suddenly seemed to be "discovered," and even to become fashionable, as if no one had ever heard of them before. For a time, it became almost original to want to be rich.

The very existence of the word "Yuppie"—another of the political terms that are both maddeningly vague and hard to avoid altogether—points to the origins of the phenomenon it seeks to describe. In the United States, there have always been young professionals, and most of them have lived in cities. Only in the eighties did this come to be considered worthy enough of note to deserve a sobriquet. (That this has occurred is perhaps all the more striking in view of the fact that the supposed characteristics of Yuppies —their interest in their careers, their interest in buying things, their jogging—are anything but flamboyantly attention-getting. It seems more surprising that these phenomena should be noticed than that they should occur.) The lineage of the term is revealed by the "ppie" ending, and proceeds, surely, from "hippie" to "yippie," and from "yippie" to "Yuppie." Had there not once been hippies, who dropped out of established institutions and tried to live outside them, and yippies, who protested against the activities of established institutions, it seems unlikely that anyone would have noticed the existence of Yuppies, who are notable mainly because they do neither—to everyone's apparent

surprise. In other words, a Yuppie is someone who has decided against being a hippie or a yippie. The almost purely
negative meaning of the term is underscored by its pejorative overtones, which include implications of shallowness,
materialism, greed, political apathy, and lack of imagination.
Hippies and yippies were not generally popular when they
existed, but they have attained an implied, retrospective
popularity in the negative implications of the word "Yuppie." Many people point to others as Yuppies; few claim the
title for themselves. The fact that the Yuppie is considered
a prime political phenomenon—a class large enough to be
given attention by vote-seekers—suggests a further negative
significance of the word. If the Yuppie is not a hippie or a
yippie, neither is he a blue-collar worker. To judge by the
campaign of 1984, the political fortunes of blue-collar workers—so avidly courted even in very recent times in American politics—had sunk drastically. Their only appearance as
a class in the 1984 election was as a ball and chain hobbling
Walter Mondale: he was viewed as over-obligated to trade
unions, which were seen not as representatives of a great
mass of people but as a "special interest."

The youthful rebellion of the sixties occurred amid
unprecedented affluence. It may be that no generation in
history has been less concerned with economic security
than the young—especially the college-educated young—
of that time. If young people in the ensuing decades were
amazed to discover things that few people in any other times
had lost sight of—that to live it is necessary to have money,
and that to have money it is necessary, unless one is born
rich, to work—and if those discoveries have precipitated an
about-face in the thinking of some of them, and if society at
large, too, is so struck by the phenomenon of suited young
people (women now as well as men) seeking employment
and advancement, then surely one reason is that in the 1960s
these hitherto universal features of human life were, for a
giddy moment, believed by millions of people to belong to

the past, and were forgotten. (These features of life, of course, were not forgotten by other millions of people—probably a majority—who knew themselves to be still regulated by the laws of economic necessity. But even these people may have entertained the belief that the days of economic hardship were numbered by economic growth, which seemed to many to have no inherent limit.) Statistics offer support for this economic interpretation. Between 1950 and 1973, average real income (measured in 1984 dollars) for families with two children rose from $14,000 to $28,000, but between 1973 and 1984 the figure actually dropped—to $26,000. Also, whereas in 1949 a thirty-year-old male could expect his earnings to increase, after adjusting for inflation, by 63 percent over the next decade, and in 1959 a thirty-year-old male could anticipate an increase of 49 percent over the next decade, by 1973 a thirty-year-old male would have to assume a 1 percent decline in earnings in the following ten years. At just the moment that a significant part of a generation started to act as if it were the first in human history to be released from the bonds of economic necessity (a belief buttressed by the government-sponsored conviction that poverty could now be eliminated from the United States almost painlessly), an economic downturn was beginning. The magnitude of the downturn was not great—it was nothing like the Great Depression, for example—but the expectations of unending economic growth that it dashed were great, and the political consequences, too, it appears, were great.

WHEN MARK GOFF, the home secretary to Representative Jim Moody, who represented the Fifth District, which contains Sherman Park, was ten years old, he was given his first bicycle—a three-speed Schwinn with fat tires and gleaming silver fenders. Goff was living with his mother in a tough, blue-collar factory neighborhood on the south side of Milwaukee, and he did not like living there. His father had died in 1948, when he was a year old, and shortly thereafter his mother, unable any longer to afford to live in the suburb of Whitefish Bay, in which the family had bought a house, moved to the south side, where she had grown up and where relatives still lived. "We were struggling," Goff told me one day in mid-October as he drove us through that neighborhood. He was giving me a tour of several parts of the city. "I knew I didn't belong here," he went on. "Our family was well spoken and well educated; we were definitely middle class. This was a rough area—there were gangs of greasers; it was Lunch-Bucket City. I had not been taught to enjoy violence." Goff was a slender man with straight brown hair, boyish features, and the self-effacing manner of many political aides. He also possessed the voluminous, detailed political knowledge found in the best of those aides. On his belt was a pager by which he could be summoned to telephone Moody's downtown office; when used, it gave off a low, discreet hum—more a vibration than an actual buzz. Having lived among working-class families, Goff went on to tell me, he had suddenly found himself pushed up into the middle class when his mother sent him to a parochial high school attended mostly by children of middle-class parents; by then, however, he had learned through hard knocks and diligent application to act in a tough, working-class way, and once again he found himself a misfit. "I just didn't know who I was," he remarked to me. At age twelve, while he was still in elementary school, the bicycle offered a means of escape. He decided that summer to cycle through every part of Milwaukee. "I decided that I was going to learn the city —just like that," he said. "Every morning, I would sit down with a map and lay out my route. I wanted to know what the city was all about—to know what was out there. I knew I didn't belong where I was. In a way, I was trying to find my roots."

Twenty-two years after the twelve-year-old boy crisscrossed the city on his bicycle, Goff had repeated a good part of the experience, this time on foot. He had been acting as advance man for Jim Moody, then a state senator, who had decided that the best way to win the Democratic primary in the Fifth District was to visit every house of a primary voter that he could. In all, he and Goff had visited about twenty-four thousand houses out of perhaps sixty thousand. It had taken fifteen months, and Moody had won the primary, and he went on to win the general election. Goff's job had been to herald the candidate's arrival. As we travelled through Goff's old neighborhood on the south side, he pointed out its characteristic "Polish flats," whose bottom floor is half underground, with windows reaching to ground level, and whose upper story is reached by a stoop. They were built as single-family dwellings; the family would live upstairs and rent the downstairs or use it as a parlor for entertaining guests. But when the children grew up they would often be given the downstairs to live in. We went north through a neighborhood called Story Parkway— "mostly Irish; flicks back and forth politically; went for Reagan in '80," Goff informed me—and came to Grant Boulevard, in the heart of the Sherman Park neighborhood. The boulevard was lined with large, gracious two-story or three-story houses, many of which were slightly run-down. Some of them, Goff told me, were the homes of the liberal activists for which Sherman Park was notable. Pointing to one house, he said, "There is an Irish family there that has adopted a black kid. That's typical." We went west, out of Sherman Park and into a more modest neighborhood, consisting mostly of bungalows. Suddenly Goff brought the car to a halt in front of a small bungalow. It hardly seemed distinguishable from any of hundreds of others that we had just passed, but it was just this that had impressed him. "Now, *this* is Milwaukee," he announced happily. "This is *the* Milwaukee house. We could drive northwest for several miles and see almost nothing but houses like this." He spoke with the relish of a collector and connoisseur, as perhaps only someone who had visited twenty-four thousand houses something like this one could do. "Look at that aluminum door!" he exclaimed. "Now, this is a one-and-a-half-story aluminum-sided house. In a month, there'll be a sign on the front telling you to enter through the back door, so you won't track mud and snow through the living room. The winters in this town are killing. See how the grass has been trimmed to the millimeter? Not a weed in the whole lawn. Woe betide the ugly little blade of crabgrass that sticks its head up in *this* lawn some fair Saturday morning. Look how the bushes are also trimmed to perfection. And don't miss that low, two- or three-inch metal edging around the little garden under the window." Goff's voice rang with admiration. "That's so the dirt from the flower beds won't encroach on that little concrete path next to them," he explained. "Notice the nicely arranged tulip bed. The guy who lives here added that chain-link fence between the lawn and the sidewalk sometime in the last ten years, when the neighborhood started to 'go bad.' "

Goff began to tell me about the man he imagined living in the house. "He's fifty-four, or maybe he's sixty, about to retire from the factory. After he got out of the Army, he raised four kids in that damn house, and it's his turf, his little piece of the world. He's a nice guy. But that guy across the street"—Goff pointed to a middle-aged black man who was unloading groceries from the trunk of his car—"has got him scared out of his wits. He doesn't know where that man over there comes from or what he's doing here."

I asked Goff what, if he judged by his visits to the twenty-four thousand houses in the area, was going through the mind of the hypothetical man in the little house.

"Fear," Goff said, without hesitation.

"Fear of what?" I asked.

"Of economic insecurity, above all. He's afraid for his financial future. He's afraid that the American dream won't turn out to be what he thought it was going to be. He's afraid

that his Social Security isn't going to hold up. He's afraid
that his kids won't be able to afford a house like this one.
He's afraid that the Japanese are taking over the car industry. He's afraid that Qaddafi will get a nuclear bomb and
everything will be blown up."

"Is that last fear an active one?" I asked.

"It's just under the surface," he answered. "But it's
there. I encountered it again and again in my walking tour
with Moody. When this guy was younger, he experienced
the civil-defense scare. Now he hears about nuclear winter
from Carl Sagan. This anxiety is not in the foreground, but it
underlies the whole mood of instability."

WITH GOFF'S FORCEFULLY spoken word "fear" sounding in
my ears, I went to see Don Taylor, the president of the
Waukesha State Bank and a co-chairman of the Reagan-Bush
campaign in Wisconsin, and asked him for a Republican
view of the public's state of mind in Milwaukee.

"There's an upbeat feeling," he told me. "No one wants
to feel that he is on the way down—that all we can do is
hang on. Young people are enthusiastic. In the high school
that my son attends, here in Waukesha, one of the teachers
in the social-studies department, who is a Democrat—he's a
fine fellow, but he's an avowed Democrat—says that for the
first time an overwhelming majority of the students are for
the Republican candidate. They like Reagan. You know, no
one wants to think that everything is running out—oil,
money, environmental resources—and that's the Democratic line. They told us the oil supply was limited, but now
there's a glut. So it turns out that maybe there's *not* a limit
on the supply after all. That's the stuff kids want to hear. If I
were a kid, maybe I'd like to hear that there were no limits
on these things. Kids don't want to feel that if they strive
and succeed that means they'll be depriving someone else.
They want to feel that everything's going up. My articulation

of the general mood is: All of a sudden, there's a future."
Taylor was sitting at his desk in his bank. When I had been
told that he was the president of the bank, I had expected
hushed office suites, heavy draperies, and cordons of secre-
taries murmuring, "Mr. Taylor is ready to see you now."
Instead, I found him in the lobby of the bank with the other
bank officers, seated at a desk, in no way different from
theirs, that stood up against a waist-high barrier dividing the
officers from the teller area, and I had only to walk up to him
to meet him. He was a thin man in his early fifties, and he
was wearing horn-rimmed glasses, a blue blazer, and brown
slacks. On his desk were a plaque that read "Don L. Taylor,
President" and a jar of jelly beans. Plate-glass windows on
three sides of the lobby gave a view of traffic speeding by
on two sides and of a parking lot, in which people in cars
were lined up to do business at drive-in windows. Taylor,
who grew up in Waukesha, and is part American Indian, had
succeeded his father, the bank's founder, as its president.
He had always been a deeply convinced Republican. In the
early 1960s, he had become disillusioned with the Presby-
terian church he had been attending and alarmed by what
he saw as a wholesale collapse of moral standards in American society, and had joined a nondenominational church—
the Elmbrook Church—in Waukesha. "I see the breaking of
all the Commandments," he said to me darkly. "Starting
with the First: 'Thou shalt have no other gods before me.'"
Taylor gave me a significant look while speaking the words
of the First Commandment, as if to say that sometimes people forgot to mention that one. "I see adultery, stealing, and
false witness. And the one most often violated is 'Thou shalt
not covet.' This is broken almost as a way of life. You also
see flagrant violation of sexual morality—but that's actually
just more coveting. At our church, we have a half-hour TV
show, and a man as senior pastor—Stuart Briscoe—who in
my opinion is the best expositor of the Bible in the world.
He's so eloquent! There's an excitement just to being in

church. It's vital, alive, full of promise. It reminds me of the Reagan campaign."

In his free time, Taylor was working on a historical novel, "in the style of Hardy," he said. "Hardy picked southern England," he explained. "I've picked Waukesha. It will be a love story—no politics in it—and I'm calling it 'The Prairieville Storekeeper.'"

I told Taylor of Goff's description of the average voter's fearful state of mind, and remarked that it was far different from his own notion of an almost euphoric public mood. I asked if he noticed any fear or worry among the voters.

"I don't pick that up," he said. "I mean, I do see some of the things he's talking about. I'm not going to sit here and tell you that the glass is completely full. But the only thing the Democrats talk about is raising taxes, and the people aren't going to buy it. They don't want to hear that."

I asked whether, as a banker, he was worried about the budget deficit, which the Democratic plan to raise taxes was designed to reduce.

"At least in the short run, I see no connection with taxes," he said. "As a long-range problem, the deficit is serious, however."

"Do you think that people have the threat of nuclear war on their minds?" I asked.

"In this community, it's not a dreaded cloud," he said. "The reaction to that movie on television 'The Day After' was that people didn't watch it in the first place. They just turned off the set. It was awfully farfetched, I thought. We're all going to die anyway."

"But isn't there a difference between one's own death and the destruction of the whole world?"

"That depends on your religious beliefs. In both cases, the Lord will decide. If He wants to terminate my life, or to terminate the world, it will happen. No, I don't see any difference. It's all in God's hands. The world is His creation, and whatever He wants to do with it is O.K. with me. If I were in His position, the world would have terminated long ago." Taylor smiled pleasantly, and shook his head. "From what I know of Sodom and Gomorrah, they weren't worse than what we see today." He reflected for a few moments. "I'll tell you a little story about the reaction to nuclear war. Last night, at about six-twenty, the sirens went off in the school building. Usually, they go off only at noon. Otherwise, it means that there's a tornado warning. And if it's not that it's a nuclear alert. But the sky was perfectly clear, so it was plain that there was no tornado. My son and I were sitting in the family room, reading. 'It *must* mean a tornado,' I said to him. 'No, I think a nuclear bomb is coming,' he said to me. Then we went back to our reading."

PESSIMISM OR OPTIMISM: a surprising choice to be asked to make in an election year, perhaps, but one that was evidently playing a crucial role in the campaign. In the mid-sixties, roughly speaking, the United States, without quite realizing it, may have reached an apogee of national self-confidence and optimism about the future. Economic growth had continued, with only minor setbacks, since the Second World War, bringing record prosperity, and the outlook for future growth, it seemed, was unbounded. Poverty in the United States, against which the President had declared "war," appeared almost an anachronism—a shameful leftover from earlier times which could be removed in short order and without any serious sacrifices by the prosperous majority. In the world at large, poor countries had come to be known as "underdeveloped" ones—countries not *yet* developed. (The poor ye always have with you; the underdeveloped you have only until they are developed.) Futurologists of the day were already beginning to wonder how the people of a "leisure society" were going to manage to spend their time after their work had been taken away from them by galloping automation. The promise of boundless economic growth was good news for the whole world, of course, but it was especially good for the United States, which held the dominant position in the world economy. Our power, too, was dominant. We had not lost a war in this century. Though in the Soviet Union we faced a fearful rival, we had the wherewithal, it appeared, to meet the challenge. Even political differences, as was suggested in *The End of Ideology,* by Daniel Bell, were likely, many people thought, to be left behind in the surge of technical progress. Nuclear weapons, it was true, shadowed this scene with their menace, but somehow they were not a preoccupation. Both the "ban the bomb" movement of the late fifties and the Cuban missile crisis of 1962 had sunk into memory.

In the seventies and the eighties, this hopeful outlook was considerably dimmed by the appearance on the horizon of what seemed to many people to be fundamental limits. The Democrats in 1984 rejected the Republicans' characterization of them as "pessimists," but it would be hard to deny that in the last decade or so they had embraced a philosophy in which the idea of limits was prominent. The Vietnam War, the national leadership of the Democratic Party had come to believe, had shown the limits on the effectiveness of military intervention in the internal affairs of other countries. Damage to the natural world had shown the limits on the natural world's ability to withstand pollution injected into it by human activities, including, above all, industrial production. The energy crisis and other scarcities showed that natural resources were limited, and would one day run out. Finally, nuclear weapons had brought mankind up against the ultimate limit—its mortality as a species—and had placed an insuperable obstacle in the way of the use of force as a means of settling global disputes with other great powers. It was thoroughly consistent with this philosophy of limits that when the federal budget deficit rose to nearly $200 billion it was the Democrats and not the Republicans who proposed painful measures, such as increased taxes, to deal with it, foreseeing economic disaster if nothing was done.

The Republicans under President Reagan explicitly or implicitly rejected the existence of every one of the limits that the Democrats had accepted as real. What the Democrats saw as actualities that had to be faced, even at great cost, the Republicans saw as phantoms produced by a defeatist mentality. The notion of limits on the usefulness of military intervention—the so-called "lesson" of Vietnam—was actually weakness, a "loss of nerve," they said. The ecological limits, while perhaps having some reality, had been greatly overstated, and the need of the moment was to liberate free enterprise from excessive regulation, environmental and otherwise. Nuclear missiles, while admittedly fearsome, were not as powerful, or as paralyzing militarily, as the Democrats said, and, in any case, could be defended against with the President's Strategic Defense Initiative: they were a technical problem that had a technical solution. Finally, the way to reduce the budget deficit was not to increase taxes but, rather, to reduce them, while also reducing social spending, so that the economy would grow; then, according to the predictions of supply-side economics, even a lower tax rate would yield increased revenues, and the budget deficit would melt away. The Democrats' embrace of budgetary restraint and the Republican Administration's effective abandonment of it (although the Reagan Administration still paid lip service to the goal of a balanced budget by supporting a constitutional amendment to achieve it) marked the culmination of a philosophical reversal in which the Republicans, traditionally the champions of governmental prudence and austerity, became the champions of unlimited "growth" and soaring expectations, while the Democrats, traditionally the champions of spending and growth, attempted to assume the role of stern disciplinarians of the country's profligate ways. The difference in philosophy was reflected in the personalities of the two candidates.

Mondale, the son of a minister, had in him something of the scolding parent, whereas Reagan, the former movie actor, had the manner of an indulgent uncle or grandfather.

The Democrats saw great perils ahead, and feared for the consequences if no action was taken. The Republicans denied or played down the perils, and saw fear itself as the danger. (At the Republican Convention, for example, Representative Jack Kemp, of New York, had said, "Mr. Mondale and his party's platform have nothing to offer but fear: fear of the future, fear of growth, fear of global leadership." And the Republican platform stated that the Democratic Party "offers Americans redistribution instead of expansion, contraction instead of growth, and despair instead of hope.") Fundamentally, the parties disagreed not on what to do about the world's problems but on what those problems were—on what the state of the world was. As it happened, one of the most important events of the 1980s—the apparent disappearance of the energy crisis and its replacement by an oil glut—offered powerful confirmation of the Republican point of view, as Don Taylor pointed out. Of all the limits, the energy crisis of 1973, caused by the Arab nations' oil embargo, was the one that had reached most tangibly into people's lives—bringing sharply higher prices at the gasoline pumps, inflation in the economy as a whole, and, perhaps, a recession. To alleviate it, President Carter, who had thermostats lowered to sixty-five degrees in the White House, proposed the "moral equivalent of war." The 1984 campaign, observers were saying, was run on the basis of themes chosen by the candidates, and the Democrats' theme of limits was seriously discredited by the oil glut. Having seen one limit melt away—for the time being, at least— many voters in 1984 questioned the reality of the others. (To the extent that the oil glut discredited the Democrats' theme of limits and confirmed the Republicans' theme of growth without limits, Reagan's term of office can be seen as an oil-glut Presidency.)

Don Taylor found an "upbeat" atmosphere around him, whereas Mark Goff discovered a climate of "fear," and it might seem unlikely that the two men lived in the same country; but as I talked to the voters of the Sherman Park neighborhood it seemed to me that the two moods might go together. The title of two more books of the sixties—*The Affluent Society*, by John Kenneth Galbraith, and *The Arrogance of Power*, by Senator J. William Fulbright—perhaps capture the confident mood of that time. Both authors were sharply critical of government policies (to Galbraith, it seemed shortsighted that the government should not spend more on social projects when the overall wealth of the country was so great; to Fulbright, the country's use of its power to force small countries, including, above all, Vietnam, to do our will, was mistaken and wrong), but both wrote against the backdrop of assumed immense national wealth and might. The controversial word in the title of the Fulbright book was "arrogance"; the "power" was taken for granted. It was against this backdrop of confidence in the country, too, that the protests of the sixties were mounted. That the United States was powerful and rich the protesters—the "pessimists" of their day—did not doubt; they only wanted the power and the riches to be applied to different ends. (Indeed, by attributing so many of the world's ills to the United States, some of them may have implicitly exaggerated the country's power.) It is perhaps only in retrospect that we can appreciate how much confidence people in the sixties had in the future, since it is only now that we know how many reasons there were to have been more doubtful. The reasons are, of course, all of the limits and obstacles— ecological, military, economic, and political—to economic growth and the use of power that the Democrats in 1984 embraced as real and the Republicans rejected as illusory. If the "optimistic" Republicans were right, the limits could be safely overlooked, because they did not exist; if the "pessimistic" Democrats were right, reality, slighted by the Republican policies, would exact its revenge in the future. In 1984, the latter view was in political disfavor—young people, as Taylor said, clearly did not "like" to believe it—but the question at least weighed on people's minds. Just as the "pessimism" that first took hold in the late sixties developed against the background of an unparalleled national self-assurance, so it might be that the "optimism" of the eighties was being nourished by underlying fear and self-doubt.

ON THE AFTERNOON of September 26, President Reagan came to Milwaukee to speak at Old Heidelberg Park, in the well-to-do suburb of Glendale. That afternoon, the crowd—prosperously dressed, country-clubbish—filed into the private park through security gates. They were there by invitation of the Republican Party, and people without tickets were being turned away. Inside the gates was a large pavilion walled on three sides and open on the fourth, the open side looking out on a park with trees and picnic tables. Several hundred demonstrators had tried to attend, but they had been restricted by the police to a street several blocks away. In the pavilion, where long tables had been set up, further restrictions were in force; the President was to speak from a rostrum inside the pavilion, and certain people could sit at the long tables, while most other people were restricted to the park area. Around the high wooden walls of the pavilion were paintings of scenes of the native countries of some of Milwaukee's immigrant groups. An oompah band was playing, and on a platform in front of the rostrum dancers in German costumes were performing Bavarian folk dances. Later, other groups, including a mostly black group of high-school students, performed other dances. I approached a knot of teen-age boys in blazers and asked how they happened to be there. One told me that they were Reagan supporters, and that they had come from the suburb of Menomonee Falls, in a bus provided for the occasion by the

Republican Party. I asked them why they liked Reagan, and got a chorus of answers.

"I like him because he's old."

"My allowance goes further."

"He's doing better than Carter."

"He's a movie star."

"I like his hair."

I asked what they thought of Mondale.

"He doesn't know how to talk."

"I don't like Ferraro."

"He just doesn't have it."

A boy with a pale-brown complexion and brown curly hair approached the group, and said, "We need a change. Reagan has done nothin'."

The others groaned.

"Look at the facts," one said.

Another turned to me and, jerking a thumb at the newcomer, said, "He's a minority—the only one in our school. He's Mexican. That's why he goes for Mondale."

"So what *are* the facts?" the newcomer asked.

There was a silence.

"Well, he got us closer to China, didn't he?" one boy said, doubtfully.

Deciding to ask about one or two specific policies, I inquired whether they approved of Reagan's handling of the environment.

"He's been cleaning it up a little," one boy said.

I inquired what they thought about the federal budget deficit.

"There's always a budget deficit."

I asked what they thought about nuclear weapons.

"Throw 'em away."

"Reagan's getting closer to the Russians now."

"He'll be trying a freeze soon."

We became aware of a deep throbbing sound—more a shuddering of the air, at first, then a noise. Then it intensified to a low thunder. Then it became deafening. It was the fleet of helicopters carrying President Reagan and his party from the airport. The deafened crowd looked in the direction of the roar, and grew still for a moment. Invading and overwhelming the rustic park scene, the roar seemed to me to embody the unimaginable power of the Presidency in the nuclear age. A few minutes later, through a back door of the pavilion several dozen men, many dressed in what looked like paramilitary gear and carrying elaborate equipment, rushed in and began to run about. It was the national photographic press travelling with the Reagan campaign. None of the restrictions regulating everyone else applied to them; they could go anywhere, and did. Some raced down aisles between the tables of local notables, seeking camera angles. Others swarmed over the performance platform. One jumped onto the rostrum, as if he were the President, and took a reading with a light meter. Then a corps of immaculately tailored, athletic-looking young men with wires coming out of their ears entered—the Secret Service. Finally, the President—smiling, diffident, rosy-cheeked—entered through the door in the back. The crowd rose to its feet and applauded. Someone at the rostrum started to lead a chant— "U.S.A.! U.S.A.!"—and the crowd took it up for a few moments, but then, apparently not finding that slogan to its taste, switched spontaneously to "Four more years! Four more years!" Excitement in the room was high; people craned their necks to glimpse the President or touch his hand as he passed down one of the aisles.

The President gave a standard stump speech, promising a tough foreign policy, accusing the Democrats of being big spenders and taxers, complimenting the Milwaukeeans on their state and city. He called Mondale "Coach Tax Hike." He spoke of his forthcoming meeting with Gromyko, and promised to tell Gromyko that the United States was "unshakable in our commitment to freedom," and vowed, "We will never again allow America to let down its guard." He said, "You know, the people of Milwaukee are as well known for your love of good beer as the liberal Democrats are for their taxing and spending; the difference is that you know when to stop." As he spoke, the excitement in the crowd seemed to wane, and the applause at the end, though vigorous, was sedate. When the President finished, a little blond girl in ethnic dress who had been standing behind him raced forward and presented him with a bouquet of flowers. The zipper sound of still cameras in action filled the air. Flashlamps flashed, lights lit up, and, for a few moments, the cafeteria blazed with white light.

THAT EVENING, Bill, Gina, and I watched the coverage of the Reagan visit on Channel 6, the local CBS affiliate. The local reporter duly noted that only people with tickets had been invited to hear the President, and that demonstrators had been kept far away.

"It's not *fair* that only people with tickets could go to a rally for the President of the United States," Gina said.

"I agree, Gina, but from a political point of view it worked," Bill said, "because you don't see him on TV getting heckled by demonstrators."

"Well, that's why I don't trust him. He's suave. He knows all the moves."

"If Mondale and Ferraro did the same, they'd get more votes," Bill said. "Just think of the Mondale appearance we saw where there were all those demonstrators yelling at him." Recently, Mondale had been heckled by Reagan supporters at a number of his campaign appearances. "Reagan looked a lot better. The fact that he sent tickets out was bad publicity, but it was overshadowed politically by the favorable image we saw." Bill spoke as if it gave him satisfaction to regard the campaign in this coolly strategic light.

· · ·

IF THERE WAS ONE thing that the two parties agreed on in this election year, it was on how sharply they disagreed. The preamble to the Democratic platform said that "a fundamental choice awaits America—a choice between two futures." Reagan said that Mondale and Geraldine Ferraro were "so far left they've left America." The Republican Party platform described the election as a choice "between two diametrically opposed visions of what America should be." Labelling the Democrats with "d" words—doom, despair, defeatism, decline, and so on—was standard Republican rhetoric. "The nightmare years" was a standard description of the Carter period. Any voter who took the claims of either party seriously probably would have had to conclude that the other party was, at best, out of its mind or, at worst, deliberately bent on destroying the Republic. And if these opinions were shared by the public as a whole one would have expected to find rancor, insult, mutual incomprehension, and contempt in people's political discussions. But I encountered no feelings of this kind among any of the people I talked to in Milwaukee about the election. No one was angry at anyone else or contemptuous of anyone else. No one thought that anyone else was disloyal to the country. No one thought that anyone else should be beaten up, or sent to Russia, or thrown in jail. (Even the opponents of abortion, who were ready to go to great lengths to illegalize it, temporized on the subject of jail sentences.) Instead, I found a broad and deep spirit of tolerance—almost a will to find agreement, or, at least, to make light of disagreement. I encountered no fanaticism in Milwaukee. On the contrary, people's views tended, if anything, to be muted, amorphous, and mild. People of different views were close friends— sometimes, as in the case of Bill and Gina, they were married to each other. The friendships and the marriages always easily transcended the political differences. And yet people did not seem to have arrived at some happy political middle ground, as if they had split the difference between the two parties. Rather, the views of each party found their reflection in people's thinking, but the differences failed to generate conflict.

This was true not only between family members and friends who held different views but also within the minds of individuals. Just as there was no rancor when two people disagreed, there was no tension when one person found himself attracted by two opposing views. Fred Skoretsky had once voted for the Socialist Workers candidate Peter Camejo and now intended to vote for President Reagan, but he saw little conflict between these positions; to him, there was an underlying continuity. Paul Toruncyk still regarded himself as a liberal yet found himself at the same time looking at that liberalism from without and calling it "tired old liberalism." John Carlton, the former McGovern activist, was going to vote for Reagan but mused that if people who opposed his policies rejected "this nonsense" it might have an effect. Even in Bill, who strongly believed in his conservative principles, the pull of liberalism made itself felt—as when, hearing Gina disagree with him, he would sometimes say, "I agree with that." At those times, I felt he was giving expression to ideas that had become dim embers in his mind but could flare up again, albeit weakly, when they were fanned by another person. Listening to the politicians, one would have found it hard to imagine how anyone could be in a state of indecision between the two candidates—how anyone's opinion could be so unformed as to swing so easily between violently opposed political philosophies. But as I listened to the voters in Sherman Park I found that many— in fact, most—of them were pulled in both directions at once. Usually, the process of internal deliberation did not seem to take the form of a debate, as on "balanced" television discussions; rather, people seemed to entertain new views as a sort of unit even as they held to old ones, much as when one is listening to the radio while driving through the countryside a new station may start making itself heard at the same point on the dial as the station one is already listening to, until the second station finally drowns out the first.

ON THE NIGHT OF THE first national debate between Reagan and Mondale, Gina, Bill, his sister Kate, and I gathered in the Gapolinskys' living room. Kate was a tall, ample woman whose rapid flow of conversation was often punctuated by a quick, sweet, self-deprecating smile. Her hair was cut straight and short, and she was wearing a voluminous blue corduroy maternity dress. When she arrived, she put on a pair of gray slippers that were shaped like elephants, with trunks and ears and faces looking straight up from the toes. She curled up on the couch next to Bill. As the debate began, Bill rested a hand lightly on one of her elephant slippers; then, for a few moments, he rested his head on her shoulder. They seemed entirely at ease with one another, as people sometimes are who have grown up together in a close and affectionate family.

In the debate, which concerned domestic policy, Reagan appeared to have lost his usual affable poise: on several occasions, he stumbled in his speech and seemed at a loss for words. Mondale, on the other hand, appeared self-confident and in command of his arguments and facts. When the debate was over, these differences in performance seemed to weigh more heavily with the company than any substantive arguments made. For Bill, the impression that he imagined Reagan must have made on others seemed almost more important than whatever impression Reagan had made on him, and he opened our conversation by saying, "I think everyone's pretty much going to say that Mondale won." (The comments of the professional observers on television immediately after the debate, in the press the next day, and in public-opinion polls later proved him right.) "Mondale did real good," Bill added. "He kicked Reagan's ass. He was well organized and well prepared. He won hands down. Most news people and objective people would have to say that Mondale won." Bill said this in judicious tones, as if he were giving a report.

"You see?" Gina said, rubbing it in. "They took away his script and the Great Communicator fell apart."

I asked if any of them thought that the debate had revealed anything important about the two men.

"I thought it revealed that Reagan wasn't as good a politician as I thought he was," Bill said.

"Do you think he perhaps just had an off night?" I asked.

"If you're going to be President for four years, you shouldn't have an off night like that," Bill answered severely.

I asked what they thought of Mondale.

"I was a lukewarm supporter, and now I'm an enthusiastic one," Kate said.

"As I've said, if Mondale could do everything he said he would do I'd vote for him," Bill said. "The big thing is the deficit. But I just don't think there's any way that anyone is going to vote to raise taxes to close it. Mondale can't do that, because the country is run by the rich. Reagan succeeds because he sees eye to eye with them. But if Mondale wipes out Reagan in the next debate I'll vote for him."

"I just hate what Reagan's doing in Nicaragua," Kate said, and Gina let out a big groan. She always did this when Nicaragua or El Salvador was mentioned. The conversation turned to foreign policy.

"Reagan thinks that as soon as those Commies get control of some little country they'll spread to more and more countries, and the next thing you know *we'll* be Communists," Gina said scornfully, adding, "That's old, disproven thinking."

"But a lot of people believe that," Kate observed.

"But shouldn't someone inform the American people? First, the people in those little countries want socialism, not Communism. That's different."

"They're nationalists," Kate chimed in.

"Yeah," Bill said. "But one thing is that when Carter took over, a lot of Third World countries were our allies, and then about fifteen or twenty of them turned against us. Reagan turned that around."

"Which ones are you talking about?" Kate challenged.

"That's probably just one of my naïve opinions," Bill said. "I'm in an optimistic mood, so when I read in the paper that our country is more respected I believe it. In the Carter period, one of my professors—a Democrat—said it was kind of disappointing how we were losing all our allies. He had a whole list of countries. Reagan built up our forces, and went into a couple of countries, such as Lebanon and Grenada, and whether or not it was good for America in every case in the short run I think it was good in the long run, because it shows people that if we see some aggression we don't like we're going to do more than just pull out of the Olympics. I thought that that was a silly and embarrassing thing for us to do—a really poor decision by Carter."

"Our policy is just to back anyone who says he'll protect our interests," Kate put in. "As long as they'll give us the resources we want, we don't care what they do with their own people."

"As long as we get our resources, we don't care even if they repress their people, or torture and kill them, or drop them out of helicopters into volcanoes," Gina said.

"Don't exaggerate," Kate said, with a smile. "I'm glad I get to say that first," she added. Apparently, she was used to being the first one reproached for exaggeration.

"I'm not exaggerating," Gina said. "The guy who preceded the Sandinistas—you know, Somoza—really used to do that to people who opposed his policies."

"Oh, well, I'm not going to vote for Reagan, because

Somoza dropped people into volcanoes," Bill said, with heavy sarcasm.

"The United States is missing the boat on a lot of things," Gina continued. "We should want what the majority wants, not what the tiny élites want. Socialism would be better for these people."

"Hell, *Communism* would be better," Bill said.

"I'm not *saying* Communism—I'm saying socialism," Gina said. "And that's different."

"But *I'm* saying that even *Communism* would be better. Maybe eighty or ninety percent of those people are repressed. Even so, maybe we have to support the present governments, which are friendly to us."

"We should let people make their own mistakes," Kate said. "That's what I like to do. I don't want anyone telling me what to do. But that's what we've been doing for centuries with these other countries. We think we know better."

"Oh, yes, you're right," Bill said. "From a human-rights point of view, I know that you're right. It's like with nuclear weapons. I know that we have enough nukes to blow up the world forty-four times and that we should never use them, and should get rid of them. But *I know better.* From an American self-interested, survival point of view, I'd rather see us run their countries. If we don't repress these countries, we'll lose them as allies. Then, before you know it, it will be just us against the rest of the world. It'll be a hundred and seventy-five to one."

"I remember seeing some TV movie in which the CIA was going to overthrow the governments of about three countries," Kate said, "and someone in the movie said that the public would be shocked if it knew. But someone else said the public wouldn't be shocked; they would be glad. I bet that ninety percent of the people would agree to anything if that's what it took to continue their life style. They wouldn't care what was happening to other countries. I often wonder: Would I share my last rations with someone if I was dying? I just don't know."

"But that's simplistic," said Gina. "It's not a choice between taking over all these countries and having the whole world turn against us. You can compromise. That's what I like about Mondale. He knows how to get things done with compromise."

"The way I see it, there's a continuum," Bill said. "Let's say it's zero to a hundred. Everything depends on where you are on it. Zero is 'We only worry about ourselves and leave the rest of the world alone.' We help only our own people, spend all our money on good things, making sure our parks are in good shape and stuff like that. We wouldn't spend any money on weapons. There's *no way* we would have to kill anyone, or have any nuclear weapons, or take over anyone else's country. A hundred is 'We take over the world.' It all depends on where you are on the continuum. But a real righteous Christian can't be President. He'd never get in. He'd just get ripped apart. I'd just love to have the country run by righteous, trustworthy, good people. But they'd be torn to pieces. They couldn't run the country, and couldn't get in power in the first place. Look at the National Rifle Association. Why does it exist? And why is it so powerful? A majority of the people support gun control, but it will never happen. Never. That's America. That's business. Business *is* the country. When business does well, the country does well. Money runs the country. You know, politicians have to say, 'I don't agree with that— that's immoral—but I'll make a deal with you. I'll support this bad thing if you support me in this good thing.' That's the part I hate about politics and business. But that's the way it is."

FOR SHOPPERS, BATHED in Muzak as they glide their carts down the colorful, abundantly laden aisles, the atmosphere of a supermarket is one of soothing calm, designed to produce a feeling of dazed well-being, conducive to buying things; but for the salesmen trying to place their products on its shelves the atmosphere is one of fierce competition. There may be fifteen thousand or more products in a good-sized supermarket, and the salesmen must try to get the maximum possible shelf space for their products. "It's just so *intense*," Bill told me as we headed south on Interstate 94 the morning after the Mondale-Reagan debate, on our way to oversee some changes in the cookie shelves of several supermarkets on Milwaukee's south side. "Standard American is just miles ahead of the competition," Bill said. "I can say to the manager of the store, 'Hey, let me put up an end display and I'll give you ten percent off on Choco-Twists.' Or I can say, 'Give me that end space, and I'll give you a permanent end-display module.' When I go to a new store or chain, I go to the manager and I say, 'John, I want to emphasize to you the importance of the cookie section. The cookie section is increasing at nine percent a year in sales. So you need more space for it. And cookies contribute five or six percent of the gross profit of your store, which is a *lot,* because they only use one or two percent of your space.' For selling, you need an action plan. I say, 'John, you don't need gum and candy at the front of every checkout counter. You could put in a little snack end display on wheels.' I'm already rolling it out at the guy. He really *can't* say no. He just can't."

We turned into the parking lot of a Kohl's supermarket. Procter & Gamble, under the Duncan Hines label, was introducing a new line of "soft" cookies, creating uproar on the cookie shelves of America. The layout of the shelves and the distribution of space had to be rearranged. Sometimes—and this was the case today at several markets—all the cookies had to be taken off the shelves and put back in a different order. Cookies are sold by the "store-door" system, in which the salesmen for the major cookie companies place the cookies on the shelves and remove stale ones. (The older cookies are placed at the front of the shelf so that they will be bought first.) The Standard American truck holds more than seventy different products, and the salesman should know at a glance where in the truck each one is, how many are in a box, and how many packages of a particular item will be required to fill a gap of a certain size on a shelf.

When we entered the Kohl's, Bill proceeded immediately to a Standard American end display and cast a sharply critical eye over it. "This is lousy," he said, with a scowl. "See how the bags are all tipping at different angles, and how they're sort of squashed into one another?" Bill began to pick up the bags of cookies, which were in a disorderly row, and, snapping them at both ends in a practiced gesture, plumped them up like pillows; then he lined them up in a neat, interleaved row. He repeated the procedure for the whole rack. The effect was that of an unmade bed being made, or a messy living room being tidied up: what had previously suggested neglect and demoralization now presented itself proudly and appetizingly to the world. Bill went on to another shelf, and here his scowl gave way to a smile. "Bob did this," he said. "He's my best salesman. Just look at this fine work. Do you see how all the bags are laced together, and how they face in the same direction, toward the flow of customer traffic—where the people will be just coming around the corner?" Bill's pleasure in the well-performed job was great. He loved to work, he worked extremely hard, and he respected the hard work of others. "I was wondering why I work hard," he once said to me. "Is it because of money? Sure, I like the money, and I need it— but that's not it. I'd work hard without the money. Do I do it for Standard American? I have an obligation to them, but that's not the reason, either. I do it because I just want to— because that's the way I am. And that's what Standard American knows about me. That's why they hire guys like me. They know that we just can't help working hard."

We met at the cookie shelves with salesmen from four other companies—Nabisco, Frito-Lay, Keebler, and Procter & Gamble. The new allocation of shelf space had already been decided, by a complicated process of negotiation, but the new plan presented a problem—an intricate puzzle—at this particular supermarket. Duncan Hines had supplied a special red plastic modular display, three feet wide, with its new line of cookies, and the manager had agreed to its use. In the natural spot for its placement, however, a pillar happened to intersect the shelf, leaving two feet on one side and one foot on the other. If the module was placed on either side, then even if the salesmen were willing to move all the cookies on the shelf, as they were, some other unacceptable result ensued—for example, the Nabisco display would be broken in the middle or Keebler would have to place its cookies across the aisle, where dishwashing supplies, not cookies, were on display. For the next two hours, the salesmen, talking together, considered at least twenty possible rearrangements of the cookie shelf, but each of them had some defect. Finally, a solution was arrived at that was satisfactory to all, but it required that a standard three-foot length of shelf be cut in two, and for that a saw was required, and so was permission from the manager of the store. After these were obtained, and the shelf was cut, by two of the salesmen, and all the cookies were rearranged in their proper places, the salesmen departed. The job had taken three hours, and had used up the lunch hour. That day, Bill skipped lunch.

In the car on the way to the next supermarket, I asked if our morning had been an unusual one.

"The problem with the shelf *was* unusual, but then there's always *something* unusual that comes up."

I asked if he ever got bored with his work.

"No," he said. "I could probably get promoted if I wanted to; I could probably go to the tower"—the corporate headquarters, in Houston. "But I'm not sure I want to. I've talked to one of the guys in my office who has been there, and he said that it was all so damned manipulative that he'd never want to go. He said it's just all politics. I'd be content to do what I'm doing now for the rest of my life."

IN LATE OCTOBER, I visited Kate and her husband, Pete, in the living room of their house, on the north side of the city. They were, in her words, "down-the-line Mondale supporters." They were better attuned to the national debate on the election as it was presented by the news media than most other people I had talked to, and they consistently took the Democratic side of the argument. When I asked why they preferred Mondale, they answered by citing at least a dozen specific issues. For example, they opposed Reagan's support of the Contra force in Nicaragua, fearing another war like the one in Vietnam; they worried that Reagan would pack the Supreme Court with justices of the far-right political persuasion; they worried that he was weakening environmental protections; they found his fear of Communism exaggerated and his defense buildup unjustified; they thought that his social policies favored the rich and were unfair to working people and the poor; they were disturbed by what they saw as a mingling of church and state represented by Republican support for prayer in the schools and by the evangelist Jerry Falwell's prominence in Republican politics. They were prepared to defend their opinion on each of these issues as well as others at length and in detail. They brought forth their views in rapid succession, alternating in speaking, as if taking turns being the spokesman for views held in common. (Listening to Pete and Kate give their opinions on this multitude of issues, I was conscious that I was hearing about most of them for the first time since I had arrived to talk to people in Milwaukee. And as it turned out, in the case of many of the issues it was also the last time I was to hear about them. In press coverage—and, to a lesser degree, in television coverage—these issues figured importantly in the campaign. In the thinking of most of the people I talked to in Milwaukee, they were more or less absent.) Their living room contained many pieces of furniture in wood, some of them made by Kate's father, who had been an expert woodworker. On the walls were several drawings of animals, and on the door was a drawing of a unicorn bearing the legend "Our faithful unicorn shall hassle whosoever disturbeth this castle." A shelf of books included several historical books—among others, *The Year of Three Kings*, by Giles St. Aubyn; *Richard III*, by Charles Ross; and *Poland*, by James A. Michener. Kate said that she loved to read historical novels—especially those set in England.

I asked them how they had made their decision about the way they were going to arrange their lives after their baby was born—to have Pete, who worked at the post office, stay at home and take care of the baby and the house, while Kate, who was also a postal worker, remained at work.

"I never did like the work at the post office," Pete said. He was a tall, thin, pale, long-limbed young man with red-rimmed glasses. He spoke in a deep, hollow voice. "In the sorting job, you have to sort fifty pieces of mail every minute, punching two numbers on a keyboard for each one. I had problems with dexterity. I'd get tired, and nervous. It can wreak havoc on your brain. Some can do it fine; others have trouble from the start. I'll try being at home for a while, and see if I go crazy without a job. Right now, I'm painting the inside of the house, getting ready for the baby's arrival."

"I have no problem with the post-office work," Kate said. "The base pay is twenty-four thousand a year, plus overtime, and I take all the overtime I can get. With Pete working, we were making about fifty-five thousand a year. It sounds like a lot, but somehow you spend it. Pete is much more ambitious and capable around the house than I ever could be. None of our friends have given us a hard time about our decision. They all understand. I guess I've always been the rebellious one in our family. As a girl, I didn't think highly of myself—I thought I was fat and unattractive. My mother helped to give me that idea, I think. I remember two distinct occasions when she said I was fat and ugly. It wasn't until years later that I got around to asking her why she had said it. She said she so much wanted me to be pretty in a conventional way. I told her it had given me an inferiority complex. Now she always says, 'You look so well.' We get along fine now. I value her more than I used to when I was fighting with her, and I want to see her more.

"It's important to my political views that I refuse to look at anyone as a stereotype. In high school, about ten percent of the kids were black, but I didn't associate with them. When I took courses in history at the University of Wisconsin, I met guys with long hair, and some of those fellows were nice. They're no different from me, I thought. Then, in the post office about thirty or forty percent are black. Working with them, especially on overtime, I realized, Hey, these are nice people, too. Some of my closest confidants now are blacks. Once, a white guy at the post office came up to me and said, 'The word is out that you like black guys.' I told him to get lost. Later, I made friends with two guys who are gay, and the same guy came up again and said, 'We see that you are talking with gay guys.' And I said, 'So I'm gay now?' The fact is, I don't like anybody telling me who I can talk to or who my friends should be."

"ST. MARY'S WAS A real neighborhood," Lawrence Kenny, Gina's eighth-grade teacher at St. Mary of Czestochowa School, who was now a Milwaukee County supervisor, told me one day when I went to visit him in his office, in the county courthouse—a massive, gloomy, pillared, mausoleumlike structure that looms over downtown Milwaukee from a perch on a hill. Kenny was a short, slightly plump man of thirty-seven years, with a plump person's large face, out of the center of which, however, peered the features of a lean person—strong, thin lips that spread in a tight, toothy smile, a sharp-looking mustache, and watchful, dotlike eyes. He was wearing a blue blazer, and a blue-and-white striped embossed tie tied in a wide knot. As a young man teaching school, he had watched the transformation of the Milwaukee neighborhoods that the Gapolinsky children and Gina had lived in.

"St. Mary's, at the time I was teaching there, was a neighborhood where you were born and where you died," he said. "It was a working-class neighborhood, near a lot of factories—American Motors, Coke, a couple of others. People married other people in the neighborhood. Grandma would live in the same building or on the same block. Maybe she owned a duplex and rented it to the family for fifty dollars a month, or maybe she wouldn't accept any money. The kids were nonprofessional—most didn't go to college. The idea was to date a girl from the neighborhood, get married to her, and stay there. It was pretty much solidly Democratic. I liked that kind of neighborhood. I grew up in strong neighborhoods in Chicago. We didn't ask whether someone was on the North Side or the South Side; we'd ask, 'What parish are you in?' But it didn't last. Every three years or so, we'd move farther southwest as the neighborhoods turned black."

Kenny had hoped that the St. Mary's neighborhood would last longer than the ones he grew up in in Chicago, but his hope was disappointed. The subversive force this time, as he saw it, was a period in American life—the 1960s, whose effects on the neighborhood he watched with some dismay. "When the sixties hit, salaries started to go way up," he said. "Union salaries at places like the Miller brewery rose from something like four dollars an hour to something like fifteen dollars an hour. There was a great accumulation of wealth. People started buying land up north and putting a shack on it—a second home—and going deer hunting. They began moving to the suburbs, or many of the kids moved to where Gina is now. Racial problems began. In the first week I was there, a kid was stabbed to death in a fight over a watch. When I was teaching at St. Mary's, there were four hundred and fifty kids there; now there are only about a hundred and twenty-five. The neighborhood lost its stability. TV had a lot to do with it. The message TV started to bring was 'Society is moving on; you should climb up the ladder': upward mobility. Now few of the old families are left. The educational philosophy was changing, too. The old ways were very simple: if one kid on the bus misbehaved, everyone was in trouble. They didn't teach values; they taught catechism. I tried to establish relationships with the kids and get them to think for themselves—to make them apply religious values to society rather than just remember what they learned in Sunday school about God. On TV, 'Ozzie and Harriet' disappeared from the screen. In that program, when their son Dave got married he stayed within earshot. But the freeways were coming, and people could commute from other neighborhoods. The old attitude of parents was 'What's good enough for us is good enough for our children,' but in the late sixties they abandoned this attitude and began pushing their kids to go to college. The schools also pushed people in this direction. People began to think that to survive you had to get a degree. I know I stressed education to the kids around then. 'If you want to be a bum, you can always do that,' I told them. 'But with an education you can also choose to be a doctor.' "

I asked whom he preferred in the Presidential race.

"Most likely, I'll vote for Mondale," he said. "But I would have preferred Hart. The Democrats have allowed the special interests to go too far."

"THERE ARE SOME things that I like about Reagan and some that I don't," Gina's brother Harry Bellacchio told me a week before the election, when I met with him, his wife, Pat, and Gina and Bill for dinner at Tom Foolery, the combined restaurant, discothèque, and video arcade that Gina and Bill had once frequented. Harry was a plump man of thirty-nine with gentle brown eyes, and he was wearing bluejeans and a dark-blue shirt with vertical pleats around the shoulders. Pat—his second wife—had large eyes and punk-style short hair with a small, two-inch tail at the back, and was wearing bluejeans and a soft-pink sweater. Gina had told me that she had spoken to Harry a few weeks before and that he was a rock-solid supporter of Mondale, because he despised Reagan's anti-unionism. "The country is in a better mood," Harry continued. "My son, who's in the Army, sees that. He gets more respect. There's more pride in the country. The person on the street feels that the United States can do great things again."

As Harry spoke, in measured, punditlike tones, Gina's face assumed a theatrical look of surprise and disgust.

"The only part that scares me is Latin America," he went on. "I don't think we should support dictators just because they're anti-Communist. You know—regimes that torture people and make them disappear. That's not the American way. And I don't like the Contra war. Reagan is a union-buster, but otherwise I like his economic policy. Inflation is down."

"Mondale wants to tax the upper tax bracket, but I don't think he can," Bill said. "It's never been done. Money runs the country."

"Which candidate do you prefer?" I asked.

"If you say Reagan, I'll hit you." Gina told him.

"Maybe Mondale," Harry said, with a sidelong glance at Gina. "Well, actually, maybe Reagan, I guess."

"I can't believe this," Gina said. "I'll bet all those polls showing Reagan winning in a landslide got to you."

"Oh, no," said Harry. "What changed was the economic atmosphere. This and the fact that second-term Presidents can be more effective. Also the fact that the country feels better about itself after the malaise of the Carter Administration."

"Mondale just sees everything as wrong, and wants to raise taxes and make people feel crappy," Bill said.

"I thought my sister the Yuppie would be voting Republican," Harry said.

"No way," said Gina.

"JEAN AND I HAVE a life plan," Gina's brother Art Bellacchio said, in a slow, calm voice. "The first stage was to raise our family, and we've done that. Charlie will graduate from the university next spring, and Vince is just going into the Air Force. Our second stage was to buy a house that's comfortable and that has some class, and now we've done that." Art gestured around him at his living room, which was furnished partly with pieces that were antique in style but were obviously newly made. His large two-story house, in a Cape Cod style—meaning clapboard walls with a shingled roof—was one of many in the same style in an expensive development a few miles west of the city limits. Constructed along newly built curving roads, the houses of the development offered views of one another, at close range. Art was a large man with heavy features and a slow, benign manner. His business card, which he had handed me when I arrived at his house, in the company of Gina and Bill, announced him to be the director of operations for a Datsun dealer and was made of brass and weighed about as much as a half-dollar. He wore gray slacks and a loose white shirt hanging out at the waist, Hawaiian style. "This is our dream house," he continued. "But we haven't completed the plan. The plan will be complete when I retire, at age fifty-five. Now I'm forty-two."

His wife, Jean, who was sitting across from him, nodded in agreement. She was thin and nervous-looking, with a friendly twinkle in her eye. "I've come a long way," she said. "I grew up in northern Michigan, in a shack with no electricity or running water. The shack was at the top of a hill, and we moved it to the bottom. We had chickens running all over the place. I learned to drive in the fields around the shack. Once, when I was driving along, I went right into an old house foundation. Boom! One second it was fields, grass, and sky all around. The next second it was dirt two inches way from my nose. My father did a little bit of everything. He was a very resourceful man."

"He was," Art said. "Jean and I married when I was nineteen and she was eighteen. I used to go out with her dad and cut down disused power lines, burn off the rubber, and sell the wire."

"We're loners," Jean said. "We worked hard."

"We didn't go to the movies or out to dinner," Art said. "We rarely had friends for dinner. We worked different shifts—while one was working, the other took care of the kids. One thing I know is: Always stay close to your family. If you fall out with them, what have you got? Our grandparents were poor economically, yet they were rich. They devoted themselves to their family."

I asked Art whom he favored in the election.

"I know which way I'm leaning," he said. "Things are going so well now it's hard not to go with the guy who is doing the winning, but I have a great distaste for this federal deficit. We owe an awful lot of money as a country—it's not just a ham sandwich. What makes sense to me is to pay back your debts a little at a time, and not have to pay the piper later. So that's why I'm leaning toward Mondale. I'm willing to pay more taxes to pay off the deficit."

Art took me on a tour of the house. All the furnishings and appliances were new and shining. When we reached the upstairs bathroom, which Art had saved for last, he said, "I want to show you something special." He drew my attention to the faucet in the bathtub, which was golden and was shaped like a swan's downward-curving neck. Looking at it, he said, "An uneducated person like me could not have achieved everything I've achieved without the help of a wonderful woman. Jean is the most wonderful thing that ever happened to me. The way she grew up, I wanted her to

have the finest available. I owe everything to her. This faucet is gold-plated. Guess how much it cost."

"How much?"

"Twelve hundred dollars." He smiled contentedly. "As
for me, though, I prefer a shower."

WHEREVER I WENT in Milwaukee, I talked to people about
politics, but I found little evidence that people talked about
politics among themselves. The day after the Mondale-
Reagan debate, none of the salesmen that Bill worked with
in the supermarkets brought the subject up. Nor did many
people seem to discuss politics within their families. Family
members very often did not know how other family members were voting. Gina had thought that Harry would vote
Democratic and that Art would vote Republican, but just the
reverse seemed to be the case, and Harry had mistakenly
thought that his "Yuppie" sister meant to vote Republican.
Even Fred Skoretsky, who took a lively interest in politics,
was surprised to learn that his wife had voted for Reagan in
the 1980 election. (However, the Skoretskys did discuss political matters with some of their neighbors.) Friends were
not necessarily better informed about one another's views.
Gina regarded Paul and Betty Toruncyk as quintessential
highly educated young Democrats when in fact they were
leaning toward Reagan.

If this lack of discussion reflected lack of interest, it also
reflected, I felt, fear of dissension. Often, other people's political views were not merely unsought but actively avoided,
or held secret. On occasion, I heard a political discussion
begin only to be abruptly dropped when it became clear that
there was disagreement among the participants. Once, at a
family gathering at Gina and Bill's house, the conversation
turned, at my instigation, to the election, and one cousin,
who worked in a car factory, expressed the view that only
two categories of people voted Republican—either "the

very rich, who are going to profit, or the very stupid, who don't know any better." After he had said this three or four times, another cousin's husband, who was a business executive, replied testily that this view displayed an ignorance of how Reagan's policies were helping the economy, by providing incentives for business to expand. A silence fell, and the subject was dropped. Those present seemed to feel that the gulf between the two views was too wide to be bridged, or even further exposed, without a serious quarrel, which might ruin the occasion. Often, I felt that in their conversations people were ready to go to great lengths to avoid dispute. Sensing that the realm of political views could be a battlefield, they shunned it. It was never quite clear, therefore, when people were steering clear of political discussions whether they did so because they were bored with politics or because they were afraid of it, or both. Gina and Bill were the great exceptions. They not only were unafraid of political disagreement but seemed to enjoy it. Yet they rarely discussed politics, they told me, when I wasn't asking them to.

Spontaneous political discussions were only one of many things that were notable by their absence in my conversations in Milwaukee. Bill and Gina were the grandchildren of immigrants from Poland and Italy, but neither of them ever mentioned either of these countries or seemed to be influenced by their national traditions. Once, when Gina saw a documentary about the Solidarity movement in Poland, she was amazed. "They all looked like Bill," she said to me. Nor did anyone else I met seem to attach importance to his or her ethnic past. Milwaukee has one of the most unusual political histories of any city in America. For thirty-eight years between 1910 and 1960 it was run by the Socialist Party, whose roots went back to immigrants from Germany who had participated in the revolution of 1848 there. But no voter I met ever mentioned this piece of history. With the exception of Kate and Pete, no one mentioned that his or her political views had been influenced by a book. And, again with the exception of Kate and Pete, and of the Skoretskys, who paid close attention to the views of several Catholic publications, no one mentioned being influenced by anything read in a magazine.

MRS. BARBARA GAPOLINSKY, the mother of Bill, Kate, Paula, and Fred, met me at the door of her brick- and aluminum-clad two-story house on the north side of Milwaukee. It was late afternoon, and a pale-tea-colored sunlight bathed the street, which was empty of people. There was no sound. Several blocks away, at an intersection, I saw an occasional car pass. Mrs. Gapolinsky was a tall, strong-looking woman with bouffant gray hair and Bill's wide, strong mouth. She was wearing a gray wool pants suit and squarish silver earrings. She invited me in to sit down in her immaculate living room, which was crowded with knickknacks. I asked her to tell me about the neighborhood when she and her husband, Thomas, had moved into it.

"Oh, it was beautiful! Beautiful!" she exclaimed with a clap of her hands. Her voice was confident and loud. She was well aware of her love of talking, and was capable of making fun of this penchant. She had told Bill that once when she was talking on the telephone to her best friend, Marge Peplinsky, she had heard a strange droning sound on the line. "Marge!" she had shouted. "Are you there? Are you asleep?" "Yes, I was," Marge had said after a few moments. "You were just so boring." Mrs. Gapolinsky had gone into gales of laughter when she told the story. Now she was saying, "We had a regular League of Nations—Polish, German, Bohemian, Irish. In a two-block area, we counted fifty-two children once. There were about eight couples who became special friends of ours. Such friends they were! On New Year's Eve, instead of going out we'd have a round-robin: we'd visit one another's houses, and have a drink at each one, and by the time you got to the eighth house, I tell you . . ." Mrs. Gapolinsky laughed heartily. "But nobody had to drive a car, so it was all right. We had a lot of barbecues, too. One couple would bring the steaks, another would bring the salad, and another the dessert. Oh, the steaks! The steaks! And then when I think of all the sewing I did. I sewed most of the children's clothes. And the baking. How I loved to bake! You know, that's what women used to do in those days. I loved it. Things are different now, though. I'm not even sure it would pay. I don't bake or sew much anymore. With the family gone, my heart isn't in it."

A photograph on the wall showed her husband and another man shaking hands. It was inscribed "Thank you, Thomas," and was signed. "That's the president of the Pabst brewery, where Thomas worked for thirty years," Mrs. Gapolinsky explained. "They gave him a watch after twenty-five years with the company. He liked the work. He was on the third shift—he left for work at eleven o'clock at night and got back at seven-thirty in the morning. He never went to work without my saying good-bye to him—except once, when I went to bed at nine-thirty. The next morning, he told me, 'Oh, was that lonesome going to work without you.' In the last year of his life, unbeknownst to me, he made plans to get onto the morning shift. He told Kate but not me. He liked surprises. He *would* be the stinker to say one night, 'Tomorrow, you have to get up at six o'clock to cook my breakfast.' But it wasn't to be. He died the month before it could happen."

With his death, the brimming tide of life that had filled her days suddenly withdrew. It was in that year that all the children left the house, and she was left there alone. "It was my husband and wall-to-wall children and their friends at one moment, and then it was nothing," she told me. When her home emptied, she noticed that something similar had been happening, although more slowly, to the whole neighborhood. The veterans of the Second World War and their

wives who had settled in the neighborhood and brought up
their children there had tended to be close in age. Now the
children had grown up and were leaving, and the parents
were growing old together. Some were sick, some had left,
some had divorced, and the rest lived in twos or alone in the
houses in which they had raised their families. The boister-
ous, youthful neighborhood, with its young, gregarious couples and its new houses and its mobs of children, was now a
silent, sedate, elderly one. "Sue Krauss, down the block, has
a girl six and a boy four, but I wonder whom they have to
play with," Mrs. Gapolinsky remarked. "None of the kids
who grew up here are still here. Well, there's Charlene Mal-
zuchi. She got divorced and has moved back in with her
parents."

I asked if the people in the neighborhood took a strong
interest in politics.

"They don't discuss it much," Mrs. Gapolinsky said.
"We don't discuss it much in the family, either. In fact, I
was astounded the other day when I was talking to my older
sister and she said that one of my brothers is a Republican."

I asked her whom she thought she would vote for.

"I'll vote for Mondale," she said.

I asked why.

"Oh, I don't know. Primarily because Reagan is a Republican, I guess."

"What picture do you have of the Republicans?"

"I really couldn't say. The fact is, we've just been Democrats. I just vote Democrat. If my husband were here, he
could get into a discussion with you."

I remarked that Bill was voting Republican, and asked
what she thought her husband might have thought of that.

"He'd say that that was Bill's choice. Just the way when
Paula planned to marry outside the Catholic Church—marry
Richard Mueller—Thomas accepted it. 'As long as she's
happy,' he said."

I asked her how she spent her time these days.

"I'm very busy," she said. "Every morning, first thing, Marge Peplinsky gives me a call, and we chat. I've known her for thirty-five years. She's just checking to make sure that nothing happened during the night. She's got a new grandson. I hear all about every little cute thing he's done." She sighed, smiling. "But I have to listen, because when Thomas died, oh, boy, was I on that phone. And did the neighbors have to listen—and my children, too. Then I look at the paper. Sometimes, on Sunday morning, a friend will call around ten-thirty and I'll still be reading the paper, and I'll be a little embarrassed. And my friend will say, 'Barbara, don't feel guilty. Remember, you deserve it. After the work you've done in your life.' That's what we say to one another: we deserve it. I never miss the travel section. Thomas and I often used to go on trips. What he loved most was to drive through small towns. He adored stopping and talking to farmers—about the problems, the machinery. Small towns seem so peaceful. Let me tell you what I love to do now. I go to the drawer where I keep the maps of all the trips that Thomas and I went on. I get them out. Then I set myelf down, and I go over the routes we took, and I remember all the places we stayed—what we ate, what we did, whom we met. And sometimes I get out the books of family pictures. I'll have a good cry. At night, I often watch TV. The kids surprised me by chipping in to get me a big color set for Christmas when my old one broke down. I like 'Dynasty,' 'Knots Landing,' 'Dallas,' and movies. I don't like the programs if they get too violent, especially not at night. When there's a wind, the walls creak and the door rattles. Sometimes it's frightening being at home alone. Occasionally, the grandchildren come over. Once a month, there is a canasta night here in the neighborhood. The other day, I went with my sister to Lake Geneva to see the migrating geese and the fall colors. I go to a lot of rummage sales, and sales at department stores, too. Yesterday, I bought two coats for Bill— London Fogs they were. Originally, they were seventy-five dollars. Then they were marked down to sixty. Then they reduced that by half, to thirty, and then they took off seven dollars more. I couldn't resist. And then there's so much to do in the house. It's a good thing you came today, because tomorrow I'm going to start moving things so I can paint the living room. And the drapes upstairs need to be done. And then there's Thanksgiving coming. By the end of November, I'm going to be a very tired woman."

I VISITED MRS. MARTHA BELLACCHIO, the mother of Art, Harry, Louise, and Gina, the day after my visit with Mrs. Gapolinsky. She lived in a small one-bedroom apartment on the second floor of a wooden duplex a few blocks from the St. Mary of Czestochowa School. Louise, who had multiple sclerosis and was confined to a wheelchair, lived across the street, attended by a helper, and Mrs. Bellacchio had chosen her apartment to be near her sick daughter. The neighborhood had not been kept up since it was the thriving center of family life described to me by Lawrence Kenny. The paint on many of the houses—mostly wooden duplexes—was chipped, the asphalt shingles were cracked, the narrow margins of grass between the houses and the street were not carefully mowed or clipped. Here the hypothetical owner of the quintessential Milwaukee house pointed out to me by Mark Goff would have found a lot of work to do. On the way to the apartment, I passed several bars with the look of an earlier era—bars with dark, yellowish interiors, untouched by any gentrifying hand, at whose counters old men stared out at the world, or into their beers, at midday.

"I became more religious after I separated from my husband," Mrs. Bellacchio told me as we sat at her kitchen table. "I felt I needed all that prayer." She had remained devout. On her kitchen wall was a picture of the Last Supper; on her living-room wall was a life-size head of a handsome, long-haired Christ. The apartment was crowded with a multitude of decorative objects, among them a pottery rabbit in a pottery bed, a porcelain mermaid bearing a bowl of fruit, her tail affixed to a plate, and a pair of porcelain horses drawing a carriage bearing a real plant. Also on the kitchen wall was a sign that said "Happiness Is Being a Grandmother." Around the living room were photographs of her children and grandchildren, including one of Gina and Bill on their wedding day. Bill was grinning hugely, Gina was smiling dreamily.

As Mrs. Bellacchio remembered it, in her life there hadn't been time to think about politics or much else. Looking back over the years, she saw five decades of unbroken, exhausting labor, performed to fulfill responsibilities to other people—responsibilities that often descended on her unexpectedly and yet were willingly accepted. Now her life was mainly one of visits with her children, conversations with them and with friends on the telephone, visits to doctors, shopping, television, and prayer. When she was about nine, she told me, living in her parents' house, in Springfield, Illinois, she was required to assume household responsibilities, including a good deal of washing and ironing. She remembered ironing sometimes until two in the morning. She left school in the sixth grade. At age twenty, she married her husband, Richard, in Milwaukee, and they moved in with her aunt and uncle, in the Victorian house in which Gina grew up. When her husband left, in 1961, she not only took care of the four children herself but also worked full time, as a salesclerk in the women's-accessories department of Schuster's department store, a few blocks away; it was her first job outside her home. She worked as a salesclerk in department stores—except for one break, of six months, in which she cleaned the showcases at a bakery—for twenty-four years. Then she retired. As her aunt and uncle grew older, they became sick, and care of them fell to her. Her uncle, who was blind in his last years, died at age ninety-four, in 1973.

I asked if she had voted Republican or Democratic over the years.

"I can't remember," she answered.

I asked if she preferred one party to the other.

"Oh, I don't pay any attention to any of them," she said. "I guess I'm just for the people who are needy—especially the elderly who are on Medicare. Hospital costs have gone up so." Mrs. Bellacchio's health was good, but she had suffered minor ailments in recent years, and had visited doctors frequently under the Medicare program. "Now, maybe Reagan has been coming along a little bit in the last two years. He's more convincing. I'm not *against* Mondale, though. But I won't vote. If I do something, I like to feel that I know what I am doing. But I know that I don't know much about politics these days."

I asked if she had ever given any thought to the peril of nuclear weapons.

"Oh, I don't think they should even exist," she said. "I think all the countries should get rid of them. It's just a disaster for themselves as well as for everyone else. Everyone just seems to be trying to be more powerful than everyone else, and wipe out more people."

I asked how she occupied her days now.

"I do the rounds," she said. "I go shopping with my sister. I see my children and grandchildren. I watch TV—'The Young and the Restless,' 'General Hospital,' 'Days of Our Lives.' They're all very good. And I go to church. I'll tell you one thing: I don't get up in the morning anymore and say, 'I've got to do *this* today, I've got to do *that*.' Oh, no. Not anymore."

Dusk was falling, and Mrs. Bellacchio turned on some lights in the kitchen. We talked more about the events of her life, and she brought out a black cardboard box of family photographs, and began to take the photographs out one by one, and to comment on each. On a beaming, plump baby: "That's Harry. He was such a wonderful baby. He was hurt real bad when his dad left. He dropped out of school, because he thought he wasn't going to do well in his exams." On a handsome young man with dark wavy hair, a pencil mustache, and a relaxed smile, slung to one side: "That's my ex-husband, Richard. He worked for a while at a lot of jobs. When he became a bartender, the trouble started. He was a man that all the girls gave a second look to." With a short sniffing laugh that seemed to express annoyance, pleasure, and resignation, she went on, "He was stepping out on me, and I couldn't stand for that." On a young couple with prominent noses and solemn, sultry gazes: "That's my aunt and uncle when they were just getting married. They've passed away." On three heavy but graceful young women, with curly hair hanging loosely down their necks, like bunches of dark grapes: "That's me and two of my sisters." On two men —one short and sturdy, with broad pants that did not quite reach his ankles, and the other taller, smiling, smoking a cigar: "That's my dad and my uncle. They were such close friends. My dad's passed away, too." On a young couple standing with ramrod posture, with a look of defiant pride, he in a formal suit of nineteenth-century cut, she in a long gown of white lace: "That's Father's father and his wife in Sicily. They never came here. They're gone, too, of course."

As I walked out into the icy, clear November evening, leaving Mrs. Bellacchio looking at her family photographs, the oldest of them vanishing into yellow or brown, as if time were darkness and were claiming the last traces in memory of these people, just as it had already claimed so many of the people themselves, I found myself thinking about how swiftly things changed or passed away in the piece of American life I had been seeing in Milwaukee. I surprised myself by remembering a passage from the book *Native Realm*, a memoir by the Polish poet Czeslaw Milosz. "A country or a state should endure longer than an individual," he wrote. "At least this seems to be in keeping with the order of things. Today, however, one is constantly running across survivors of various Atlantises." The Atlantises he had in mind were whole countries and cultures that had sunk under the waves of the man-made catastrophes of European history in the first half of this century. Milwaukee in the years after the Second World War (and before, for that matter) had been unvisited by any such catastrophes; on the contrary, it had enjoyed an unbroken peace and prosperity that were rare for any community in history. Even for a city in the United States, Milwaukee was notable for its stability. I was struck by how many of the people I met there were born there, and how happy they were with life in the city. Yet I felt that, for reasons that had nothing to do with the catastrophes of history but only with quiet and peaceful yet thoroughgoing changes in the way life was lived, the city that had existed only twenty or thirty years ago was an Atlantis that had quietly slipped under the waves.

Of course, it's always tempting to regard the past as an ideal time from which the present has fallen away: back then "Our Town"; now the shopping mall. Many of the people I met were dreaming of "the old neighborhood," yet in the old neighborhoods, no doubt, people were dreaming of still older neighborhoods—and in Milwaukee, a city of immigrants and their descendants, they were probably dreaming of the old country. Still, it appeared that centrifugal forces in the city (as no doubt in other cities around the country) had been especially powerful in recent decades. There appeared to be little left of the dense overlapping of stores, offices, places of entertainment, and residences which the notion of "city life" still evokes in our minds. By and large, all those elements had been separated from one another—aggregated in residential communities, compressed into a purely commercial downtown, collected in shopping malls, or scattered in strips along highways—as if

a cake had been unbaked and returned to its original ingre-
dients. Ever since I had arrived in Milwaukee, I had been
struck by the emptiness of its streets. Each time I entered a
new neighborhood, it seemed to me, I saw houses, I saw
trees, I saw lawns, I saw cars (mostly stationary), but I saw
no people—or, at most, one or two. I wondered whether this
might simply be the reaction of someone from New York,
where the occupants of ten or twenty or fifty stories period-
ically pour down into the one story of street level, and where
in some places it is hard at lunch hour to keep your foothold
on the sidewalk. Also, it was autumn, and people could not
be expected to spend much time outside. Yet, thinking of
Mrs. Gapolinsky's description of the neighborhood in which
she and her husband had brought up their family, it seemed
to me that the look of the Milwaukee neighborhoods must
have changed; then, surely, more people would have been
out and about, and visible to the passerby: some of the fifty-
two children would have been in the yards or on the sidewalks, some of the mothers would have been coming and
going from their houses. And, of course, there had been vast
and documentable changes in American life that would be
responsible for such a change in the look of things. The
triumph of the automobile had brought about the eclipse of
the local store by the shopping center, making it virtually
impossible any longer to shop in any way but by car. The
automobile had also loosened the tie between home and job,
so that commuting to and from the workplace had to be by
car, and if the streets were empty of people one reason was
that few people any longer walked to the store, or to work.
In the same period, women were leaving the home and taking jobs. And as they left their homes and neighborhoods
their children had to be cared for elsewhere, in schools or
day-care centers. In any case, they were having fewer children, and the size of families was decreasing. With the wife
at work, having another child, which had previously meant
only having another mouth to feed (a comparatively light

economic burden), now meant withdrawing one of the family's breadwinners from the payroll, for many working women still wanted to be at home while their children were in infancy or early childhood. Almost every working woman I spoke to in Sherman Park was enthusiastic about having a job. Whether they considered themselves feminists or not (and most probably would have declined the label), they experienced their move out of the confines of the house, with its cooking, its housework, and its child care, a liberation. They enjoyed the independence, the paycheck, the friends on the job. And in a time when divorce was common many saw their jobs as insurance policies.

As women moved out of the house, the economy, it seemed, was taking over the work that previously had been done there. The clothes that Mrs. Gapolinsky would have sewn at home were now being bought with credit cards by Gina at Gimbels or Zayre, and even some of the meals that Mrs. Gapolinsky would have cooked at home were now being cooked commercially, by McDonald's or Burger King or Pizza Hut. That might account—in part, at least—for the much-mentioned rise of a "service economy." The service economy was the household turned inside out. The empty neighborhood street and the busy shopping mall went together. Seen from the vantage point of today's economy, the households of the 1950s were like cottage industries, with payment for the wife-worker coming out of the husband's paycheck. Now that tight arrangement had broken up. The wife was out of the house, employed elsewhere, and the work she had done had been standardized and centralized in the economy at large. A parallel development had occurred among old people. A structure of public and private payments—Social Security, Medicare, Medicaid, life insurance, private retirement plans—had been put in place that gave great numbers of them financial independence from their children, and so the elderly, too, were less likely than before to live with their families. More likely, they lived

alone, as Mrs. Gapolinsky and Mrs. Bellacchio did. But pre-
cisely because family ties were under stress they seemed to
stand out now with all the more clarity and poignance. I
thought of Mrs. Gapolinsky submerging her occasional
sharp disagreements with her children on how to live so that
she would not be cut off from them. I thought of Bill telling
Dale Olen and his audience that the happiest thing in his
life was hugging his wife and children. I thought of Bill with
his head on his sister Kate's shoulder watching the Reagan-
Mondale debate. I thought of Kate in her history classes,
wishing that her uneducated but bookish father could be
there with her. I thought of Mrs. Bellacchio's life of service
and work. And I thought of Art working all his life to build
his dream house so that he could present his wife with the
most beautiful bathtub faucet in the world.

In the 1950s or thereabouts, a stereotypical picture of
the American family took hold in the public imagination. In
the picture, there was a house, and in the house there was a
woman. There were also a man and children, but they came
and went: in the morning, the woman sent her children off
to school and her husband off to work (having served breakfast to all, and perhaps packed lunch for all); and in the
afternoon and in the evening she welcomed them back. To
whatever extent that that life actually existed in the United
States (and Mrs. Gapolinsky's life doesn't sound dissimilar),
it no longer does. It is an Atlantis. There is a new life there,
yet no picture of it has taken hold in the public imagination.
In the circumstances, each innovation seems like a depar-
ture from the old picture, as if in one of those games in
which one is asked to tell what is "wrong with this picture"
everything were "wrong."

The consequence for politics of this new life, which
people now live, though they have not yet quite identified
it, would appear to be as yet undetermined. Politics has
content, but it also has a texture and a shape. The dissolution
of neighborhoods, which, among other things, helped un-

dermine the party machines that thrived in those neighborhoods, is accompanied by a dissolution of political ties.
Replacing the ties based on community, as many observers
have pointed out, are ties created by the television set. Some
of the characteristics of those ties, as observers also have
pointed out, are speed of transmission of information and
mood; unprecedented breadth of reach; paucity of detail (as
compared with what is available in print); a certain "cool-
ness" and neutrality (which is, of course, embodied in law,
being required by the fairness doctrine and the equal-time
regulations that apply to broadcast media); and a "short attention span." To these, another characteristic might be
added: forgetfulness, which is symbolized by the fact that
once the image on the screen is replaced by the next one it
cannot be retrieved by the viewer.

Part of the force of the printed word stems from the fact
that in print public events, which are in themselves tran-
sient and perishable, are *fixed*—they become part of "the
record." (We speak of a "newspaper of record"; no one
would dream of speaking of a "television station of record.")
Through television, public events are magnified but
within the moment. On television, events expand instantly,
vividly, compellingly, pervading all parts of the nation at
once, but then they vanish. The tremendous political power
of television has been rightly acknowledged. Less acknowledged, perhaps, is a corresponding weakness. Television is
powerful because it can dominate the moment—reaching
and swaying the millions swiftly. It is weak because it cannot outlast the moment—cannot make an impression that
endures. This hidden weakness may account for the political mistake made by those Democrats who believed that the
Watergate crisis and the Vietnam War would determine the
political orientation of the young generation for life, much
as the Depression and the Second World War had done in
an earlier generation. Those hopes, of course, were rudely
dashed by the election of Ronald Reagan. If it were true that

political views were formed enduringly by television, then no event should have been more decisive than Watergate, for no event has ever received more television coverage; suddenly, instead of seeing two-minute clips on the news, the public was watching hour after hour of unbroken coverage. Yet just a decade later it all appeared to have become politically weightless. The Vietnam War was somewhat different. For the majority, it, like Watergate, was a television event—the "living-room war," in Michael Arlen's phrase. But for two minorities—those who passionately opposed the war, and became active in the movement to end it, and those who fought in the war, or were very close to someone who fought in it—Vietnam did become a life-changing event. The disparity in the depth of feeling between the television-watching majority, on the one hand, and the two minorities, on the other, is responsible in good measure for the peculiar pathos of that war, which first made itself felt when soldiers returning from the war found that the country that had sent them there had little interest in them or in their overwhelming experiences.

The world with which politics deals, too, has a shape, and that shape is important for the shape of politics. In a speech at the commencement at Harvard University in 1978, Aleksandr Solzhenitsyn spoke of the "pitiless crowbar of events," which wrenches into the lives of those who turn their backs on the realities of the world. In the first half of the century, the pitiless crowbar reached into American life at least twice—in the Depression and in the Second World War. In those catastrophes, millions of people lost their jobs, were driven from their homes, went hungry, or were wounded or killed. In the postwar period, the United States has not experienced such events. The pitiless crowbar has been busily at work in the world—especially in the Third World, where poverty, famine, revolution, and war have all been common—but Americans, notwithstanding our considerable social problems and our involvement in the Korean

War and the Vietnam War, have, for the most part, been spared. The wars and revolutions and famines have in every sense been "living room" events for us.

None of this is to say that the issues before us are any less momentous than those of the first half of the century; on the contrary, they are more so, for in the nuclear age more is unquestionably at stake. Nuclear war, however, would be poorly described as a pitiless crowbar. If it comes, it will not pry, crowbarlike, into our lives; it will simply and abruptly end them. And in the meantime—and that meantime has gone on for more than forty years now—it does not come; and not only does it not come but it may well protect us from large-scale conventional war as well. And the freedom from conventional threats, in turn, leaves us secure in the enjoyment of what by world standards is, in the case of a majority of us, immense wealth and comfort. If there is active complicity by the average citizen in the nuclear peril, it may lie in this: We are ready to pay for our comfort and safety by accepting the threat of our annihilation, and of the possible annihilation of mankind. The point in the present context, however, is that the shape of the peril fits into a broader pattern than our political life seems to have assumed. In this as in other respects, the lines that connect the individual citizen to the body politic and, beyond that, to the world at large, appear to have become attenuated. The parties, which in recent decades have served to help people organize their political thinking, seem to play that role less and less, and events themselves have failed to leave deep and lasting political impressions. Nor has television filled the breach: on television, it seems, the world draws closer but matters less. Commentators have spoken of a possible realignment—from the Democratic Party to the Republican. Thinking again, they have wondered whether what is happening may not in fact be de-alignment—a process in which the voters are set adrift from both parties and become independent. It is hard not to notice, however, as the number of those who do not vote at all increases, that what many people have drifted loose from is not just one party or another but politics itself. Each election year, the politicians and others in and around politics and government campaign and, as required by the Constitution, hold elections, and everyone involved gives every sign of believing that the drama is as engrossing to the country as it ever was; but the evidence grows steadily that the public at large is becoming less and less interested. It's said that recently politics is being treated more and more as if it were an entertainment. If so, the performance is a failure. Slightly less than half of the voting-age population does not vote in Presidential elections, and the somewhat more than half who do vote do not live in another country from the nonvoters; there is little indication that anyone who does not have a professional interest in politics in this country takes a very passionate interest in it. Is the American public becoming not so much de-aligned as de-politicized? Are realignment and de-alignment, for both of which the record provides evidence, part of a deeper process of de-politicization? If so, reality itself, by sparing us its ruder shocks for almost half a century, seems to have cooperated. It looks at us from behind the glass wall of the television screen, leaving us free, if we so wish, not to think about it at all—at least until such time as it bursts through the screen and vaporizes us where we sit.

AS THE ELECTION APPROACHED, Bill's flirtation with the idea of voting for Mondale faded. Reagan's performance in the second debate, in which he appeared more in command of his arguments and his facts, reassured Bill that the President was a competent politician after all, and his concurrence with Reagan's views reasserted itself. Gina remained a steadfast supporter of Mondale. Of all the people I talked to in Milwaukee, she was the least divided or wavering in her political views. Although she was not dogmatic or closed-minded, the forces that were eroding or overturning the political ideas of others—changes in economic or social circumstances, changes in political fashion, the magnetism of a political bandwagon—left her unmoved. Her rise in the world brought with it no reappraisal of her views of the poor or of the programs for helping them. The declining fortunes of "tired old liberalism" led to no crisis of doubt in her liberal beliefs. The mood of optimism and good feeling about the state of the country propagated by the Reagan campaign caused no shift in her mood or feelings. Her views, wherever they came from and however she may have arrived at them, seemed the natural and comfortable ones for her, and she showed no inclination to alter them.

Two days before the election, I sat down with Gina and Bill for a last conversation. I asked Bill how important religious faith was to him and whether it influenced his political views.

"Maybe it's not as important as it should be," he said. "Deep down, I believe. But it's just like banning the bomb. I'm too caught up in trying to survive in America, and if I have any spare time I want to spend it with Gina and the kids rather than in church. Talking to Paul Toruncyk threw me off traditional Catholicism a little. In traditional Catholicism, either you're good or you're bad, and if you're good you go to Heaven and if you're bad you go to Hell. Paul said we won't go to Hell for just one bad act—the question is whether you are a good person or not. That made me relax, because I feel that I am a good person."

"If you were more religious, where would that lead?" I asked.

"I'd have more satisfaction with my life. I'd have a morality that tells me how to run my life—what's wrong and what's right. The problem is that some of the things I'm doing in my business life would not be sanctioned by perfect Catholic faith, because I've got to lie a little, I've got to misrepresent the truth a little. In America, any businessman in any kind of competition has to do a little of that. For instance, all the supermarkets want to know how the competing supermarkets are pricing our wares in their sales, so that they can try to undercut them. So if someone at Pick 'n' Save asks me what Kohl's is charging, I'll say, 'I don't know,' even though I do know. Am I lying? Yeah. But it makes it a little easier. If I said, 'I can't tell you, for ethical business reasons,' he might say, 'Oh, yeah? Well, I'm not going to do business with you.' Some will demand to know what the competition is going to charge. But I won't tell them. The worst I'll do is say I don't know."

I asked Gina about the importance of her faith in her life.

"I hate to say it, but my life has just become too busy, and I've just about forgotten about religion," she said. "I feel like saying I feel guilty about it, but I guess I really don't. I believe in God, but I don't believe in Hell. I don't believe that anybody goes to Hell. I believe that God thinks that people are fallible."

"So we're all cool, and we'll go to Heaven anyway?" Bill asked.

"Well, I don't believe in Hell," Gina said.

"Oh, I do," Bill said. "That's part of the reason I sometimes don't do naughty things."

"Really?" Gina said. "Now, if I don't do bad things it's because I always worry how the other person would feel. *That's* being moral—not because you're afraid you're going to go to Hell. But sometimes I wonder: If there really is a God, why does He let these terrible things happen to people?"

"Just because Adam and Eve screwed up," Bill said. "So maybe you think *this* is our Hell."

"No," Gina answered. "Why does there have to be a Hell at all?"

"Some people are going through Hell right now," Bill said.

"That's true," Gina agreed.

"And you think we're going to escape all that?" Bill asked.

"I don't know. I think everybody may have his own private little Hell." Gina looked glum.

"But you do believe in God?" I asked.

"Oh, *yes*," Gina said firmly. "But I don't think it's as complex as some people like to make out. I think it's quite simple. I really believe in the one Commandment that you should treat other people the way you want to be treated."

"That's not a Commandment, it's the Golden Rule," Bill pointed out.

"Whatever. If you live by that one principle, that pretty much encompasses everything, like cheating, lying, and stealing. It's pretty simple, really."

"And is the rule important for your political views?" I asked.

"Oh, yeah, I think about it a lot. What made me born in the United States? I could have very easily been born in Nicaragua. And how would I feel if a bunch of rich Americans were taking up ninety percent of the world's wealth and telling me how I should be governed?"

"Oh, sure," Bill said. "The Golden Rule is great—when it's convenient, when it's profitable."

"I always think about how an issue is going to affect the people involved," Gina said.

"O.K.," Bill said, apparently taking her assertion as a challenge. "I just think about how an issue is going to affect *me*." Bill spoke lightly, mischievously. "And do you know what? The *reason* Gina feels she can afford *not* to think about how the issue affects her is because I *do*. It's not that I *want* to be that way; I'd like to be a morally perfect Catholic. But it's only because I am being a good, staunch businessman who can lie a little now and then and rationalize it that Gina can be so liberal and honest. Of *course* I don't want any nuclear arms and I want everyone to be equal and democratic. But if we're going to make more money than other people, and have all the crap we want, I'm going to have to be more aggressive, and be a better salesman. Otherwise, I'd be strong for welfare, and say we're all equal, we're all the same, so let's live exactly the same, and be perfectly nice to each other, whether we're gay or black or whatever."

"What's wrong with that?" Gina asked.

"There's nothing wrong with it. But I'm not going to sacrifice myself and let our family fall to a lower income level, because there's somebody right next door ready to stomp on me and take my job."

"Oh, God, don't be *ridiculous!*" Gina cried out.

"How can you deny that? This is America. There's nothing wrong with what I'm saying. The truth is, *you* won't *stand* for having anything less than we have, materially. In fact, you won't even stand for having as much as we already have, because you want more. And if you want more we got to *make* more. Or—*cut out the fat.*" Bill's voice was booming. "I mean, you have to stop buying so many clothes and stuff."

"Bill!" Gina cried out, booming back. "*That* has nothing to do with it. We're having a *political* argument, and my clothes are irrelevant. That's not fair."

"Our spending has everything to do with it. And it should."

Gina was silent.

"You can't argue with that," Bill said. "That's why you're not arguing."

Gina remained silent. After a few moments, she said, "I don't know. Maybe I *can* be a little more idealistic because I feel that he's ultimately responsible for paying the bills, and therefore he has to be more practical."

"You see? You can afford to vote your conscience because I am facing reality for you."

"*Wait* a minute. I shouldn't have agreed with that. It

makes sense, but it's not how I feel. It's logical, and it's how *some* women might feel, but not me. I take it back."

"You can't take it back."

"I take it back. The statement is withdrawn. Even if I were taking care of the kids by myself and working full time, I would believe what I now believe. It would just go against my backbone to vote just on the basis of self-interest. It's true that sometimes I think that a vote for Reagan *would* be in our interest. But I just can't even *begin* to think that way. I can't even take the first step."

ON ELECTION DAY, President Reagan defeated Walter Mondale by 54,450,603 votes to 37,573,671. In Milwaukee's Fifth District, the vote was 90,027 for Reagan, and 139,057 for Mondale. Mrs. Gapolinsky voted, as she always did, for the Democrat. Mrs. Bellacchio did not vote. Paul Toruncyk, feeling a reawakening of tired old liberalism, voted for Mondale, but his wife, Betty, voted for Reagan. Fred and Elizabeth Skoretsky, still more interested in saving the unborn baby than in banning the bomb, voted for Reagan. Harry, awash in the tide of good feeling about the country, overcame his aversion to the Administration's policy on aid to the Contras and voted for Reagan. Art, changing his mind at the last minute, voted for Reagan. Kate and Pete voted for Mondale. So did Paula and Richard Mueller. Bill's brother, Fred, voted for Reagan. Bill, casting his vote in defense of his family, voted for Reagan. And Gina, still unable to calculate her vote on the basis of her interest, voted for Mondale.

A Note on the Type

This book was set in Caledonia, a typeface designed by W(illiam) A(ddison) Dwiggins for the Mergenthaler Linotype Company in 1939. Dwiggins chose to call his new typeface Caledonia, the Roman name for Scotland, because it was inspired by the Scottish types cast about 1833 by Alexander Wilson & Son, Glasgow typefounders. However, there is a calligraphic quality about Caledonia that is totally lacking in the Wilson types. Dwiggins referred to an even earlier typeface for this "liveliness of action"—one cut around 1790 by William Martin for the printer William Bulmer. Caledonia has more weight than the Martin letters, and the bottom finishing strokes (serifs) of the letters are cut straight across, without brackets, to make sharp angles with the upright stems, thus giving a "modern face" appearance.

W. A. Dwiggins (1880–1956) began an association with the Mergenthaler Linotype Company in 1929 and over the next twenty-seven years designed a number of book types, the most interesting of which are those in the Metro series: Electra, Caledonia, Eldorado, and Falcon.

Composed by Dix Type Inc., Syracuse, New York

Printed and bound by The Haddon Craftsmen, Inc., Scranton, Pennsylvania

Binding design by Claire M. Naylon